SYMBOLS OF SEX MAGIC

Secrets from the Temple of ISIS & LILITH

Written by:

Luna Ora & The Sisters of the Temple

Mother Is Rising
The sex magic school of ISIS and LILITH.
Luna Ora
www.motherisrising.com

Written and channeled by: Luna Ora and the sisters of the temple.

* 2nd edition 2022

TO THE AWAKENED ONES:
May we return to the temple one more.
May we return to the womb of the mother.
May we unite as her divine children and birth her world into life.

CONTENTS

PART 1- ENTERING THE TEMPLE _____1

Introduction _____2

The school and Initiates _____5

What is the Temple? _____9

Walking through the Temple_____11

The Temple Sisters-_____12

The return of the Temple_____14

Connection to the Temple_____15

The Sisters speak to all humanity_____16

The Gifts of the Sisters _____18

Dreaming _____20

The pyramid_____21

PART 2- WHAT ARE SYMBOLS? _____23

What are symbols? _____24

The magic of symbols _____26

How to work with the symbols _____28

Hidden in plain sight _____30

PART 3- THE SACRED SYMBOLS _____33

The Circle_____34

The Cross_____43

Triangle/ Pyramid_____48

Star of David/ The Merkava_____54

The Chalice_____66

The Ouroboros_____73

LILITH_____87

The Ankh_____97

Spiral/ Triskelion_____104

The Diamond_____109

The 'all seeing eye'_____117

Sex Magic Numbers_____121

The number 3_____122

The number 33_____124

The number 0_____125

The number 4_____126

The number 13_____126

The number 6_____ 127

The number 9_____ 128

The number 11_____ 129

The number 22_____ 129

The number 33_____ 130

The number 8_____ 131

The number 44_____ 132

PART 4- LOVE OF THE TEMPLE_____ 133

Purification & cleansing_____ 134

Twin flames_____ 137

The story of the Twins_____ 139

The law of gender_____141

The twin soul agreement_____ 145

Walk-in Twin flame souls _____ 151

The number of twin flames on earth_____152

Create your own symbol_____154

TO THE TRUE LOVE-MAKERS_____ 155

ACKNOWLEDGMENTS

I thank my earth mother for showing me the path of a strong, free woman.
I thank the mother for embracing me into her womb with wisdom and a divine mission.
I thank all my earthly brothers and sisters- the brave ones who follow their wombs and hearts each day to embody the mother's love and power on this planet once more.
I thank the sisters of the temple for being my guide, protectors and support in dark times. I thank the truth, wisdom, knowledge and love and I thank the darkness for showing me how to defeat it. For bringing me into my light.

"Signs and symbols rule the world, not words nor laws."

Confucius

PART 1
ENTERING THE TEMPLE

INTRODUCTION

This is the knowledge of the temple.

Within the (symbolic) walls of this book are hidden occult secrets that are highly protected. They have been dug up from the ashes of our collective shadows and have been brought forth back into the consciousness of mankind.

The information and knowledge in this book are mostly channeled directly from the sisters of the Temple. The Temple of ISIS and LILITH,

LILITH is the one that holds the codes of light and information. She has been protecting all sisters since the beginning of time itself. She has been holding and guarding the true secrets of the temple until it was the right time for it to re-emerge and re-awaken in human hearts.

ISIS is the one who has been silently protecting and managing the energies of the temple itself, in the dimension that it exists still, parallel to ours, until today.

Isis, if you will, is the 'head priestess of the Temple'. The Eternal teacher and guide and healer of the ancient wisdom. She holds information within the cells of her body and intertwines it in her etheric body and energetic soul fragmentation, which she has sent out to the ether (as well as through incarnated women) until it was the right time to bring it back to our world and time. In her reality time does not exist of course. But in ours it is.

And the time is now.

The Sisters of the temple ask that you read the words in this book with an open heart and an open mind. To release all ideas or stories that you might have from other humans or dogmas about what sex is and about what a Sex Temple might be.

This information will be best understood, and you will have a deep knowing of its truth if you meditate before you read, ground yourself as much as you can, and keep your body as pure as possible. This also means in the time you are reading this book it will be most beneficial to begin a plant-based, whole foods diet, which will elevate your frequency and help you connect with the energy of this information in the best way possible. Give it a try. The worst thing that can happen is that you will be a bit healthier.

What you will read will be a combination of a direct channeling from the sisters themselves, as well as my interpretation of what they show me, which in many times is, wordless, so I am left with the task of finding the words and describing it the best way I can.

This book will contain the temple knowledge of sacred symbols as well as help you connect to the temple itself on a whole other level.
There are more sex magic secrets, tips, and knowledge hidden between the lines, so make sure to not skip any part of this book if you don't want to miss any 'juicy' parts.

The symbols chosen in this book have been chosen to be mentioned for a few reasons.
The first is that they have been holding great significance and use in the temple, so their understanding is important for those who have mastered the self- initiation period (which is the first book in this series- *Sex Magic Evolution*). If you haven't yet studied and practiced the sex magic school's first level yet, it is the time to do

so, for the knowledge provided there is not only connected to the knowledge in this book, but it helps reprogram your subconscious mind to a space where you can actually connect to the dimension of the temple and receive the wisdom that is presented here in the best way for your evolution.

The temple holds spiritual technology. Far beyond what we can grasp with the state of our collective consciousness today. I have 'translated' the teachings of the temple in the simplest terms I could for the wisdom to be fully rooted within the mind of the initiate- YOU. Symbols are used as a technology- by the temple, and today by the dark sorcerers who have been using our own energy against us. This book will give you back the hidden paths we have lost in the easiest way so that you can use them starting today. But you must remember that nature- which WE are a part of- IS THE TRUE TECHNOLOGY. We, as well as all life on the planet, hold the ultimate technology and knowledge, but in order to connect to nature, we must fully know ourselves.

This is our world, and we must take it back as well as take back all hidden knowledge that will help us transcend in this timeline, but we can only do this, if we look within, face the mirror that this reality is holding up against us and create a full divine union in ourselves, and with the world itself.

I am proud to be a servant of the mother and a bringer of this Divine Knowledge.
One of the things that the sisters of the temple have taught me, and I, in return, am teaching future priestesses of the Temple, is that knowledge must come with wisdom- which is the knowing in the most divine, wise way, of HOW and WHEN to bring and share the knowledge itself. For it is not enough to just have the knowledge by itself.

And the third piece to this puzzle, with the Knowledge and the Wisdom- is Love.

This is the sacred Trinity that any sex Priestess at any given point in her service in the temple must live by and embody- knowledge, wisdom, and love.

THE SCHOOL AND THE INITIATION

Those who cannot understand and be open to this book, will not be ready to be initiated into the temple's teachings and knowledge. They can logically understand some of the teachings but will not be able to fully embody it. This book (as well as the book – *Sex Magic Evolution*) is a preparation to hold the frequency and light codes of the temple.

THE TIME OF THE DIVINE FEMININE and THE MOTHER has arrived.
Union of the powers (divine feminine and divine masculine) is needed now more than ever. It is not even about *balancing* anymore, but a full divine *union* must occur for the awakening of our human consciousness to occur.
Many say we have time, and all is light and love. But this is not the mindset that will bring awakening because even though it is true, it is not the only truth.
It is the mindset that the dark masculine world wishes to place on the mind of humans, to keep them entranced. Many in the spiritual community are under this trance as well and are just as asleep as the 'un-spiritual' humans.

The awakening will not happen in a yoga class or following a guru. It will happen in our minds. This is a revolution of the feminine sacred blood, of the mother, of the human potential and powers and of our consciousness.

I AM A STORYTELLER...

My name is Luna. I go by other names as well, and they keep changing as I shift and evolve through the endless, different dimensions of my journey.

I was born in Israel, in a city called Haifa. I have traveled the world and have played many roles and characters in my human form.

I officially began my initiation in the temple when I was 33, though I have been in communication with the temple years before that, I just didn't know what to call this energy. I am now 36 years young writing these words.

I have been a servant of the mother for years now, but even before I found my Divine Service on this planet, I always knew I am here to serve. I always knew that my job is to change the course of destiny on this planet. In some way or another.

The information in this book is mostly channeled from The Sisters of the temple themselves.

I have been initiated for two years myself before I was ready to receive this information and share it with the world.

I have been preparing myself for this Mission since I can remember. Even before I even knew what my mission was. And my mission is still evolving and expanding every day.

I have been a performer, singer, actress, dancer, nanny, teacher, waitress, I have been a soldier in an army, I have been a traveler. I am a sex priestess in the temple of Isis and Lilith, and I initiate men and women into the true knowledge of sacred union and back into their power. But mostly, I am a storyteller.

Some of the stories I write are fiction, but even they are based on our 3rd-dimensional reality and are written with light codes meant to re-program the human psyche.

This book is also a story. Everything in life is. And it is best to see it all as a story, which we, are the constant writers of. But this story is one that is not mine. It is a story that I am receiving with the upmost honor and gratitude from my Divine Sisters of the Temple. Me telling you this is a story- doesn't make it unreal. On the contrary. Because of the fact I told you everything is a story; I have given permission to your subconscious mind to open even more and to use your own inner wisdom while reading this book's sacred knowledge. I have also tried to keep the teachings to a minimum information and maximum simplicity- because the subconscious mind works best with simplicity! So, I am now giving you the best chance to get the most out of this journey. To awaken your own light codes and find your own connection to the temple.

It is my job to keep myself- body, mind, heart, and soul- in the highest frequency always, so that I make sure that all the information I receive is clear, filled with truth and light codes, and that I know how to wisely share this information with humans, for not all information can be accepted or understood by humans at this point in our evolution. It is my job to be the 'translator', if you will, of these energies and light codes of information, and bring them to you right now in the best way that I can.

I have many stories in me that are waiting to be birthed into this reality. Stories that will change the timeline of our specific reality (like most stories do, by the way). Therefore, I have been guided to wait with my own stories (and it seems like I've been waiting for such a long time already), because this one, a story that is not mine, but one I am committed to share, and all information from the temple itself, is right now available to you- to those who are ready to awaken to their true power and live in their full divinity on planet Earth.

I call this a story because stories are the best way for humankind to receive information.
It is the best way for our subconscious mind to understand information and to process it- especially information such as this which is bombarded with high-frequency light codes- but know that though this is a 'story', it is not fiction!
This is the truth that has been hidden from us for too long, and it is time for us to receive all the tools we can to take our power back.

I do not know if there are other sisters besides Lilith and Isis who channel through me. It feels like there are. I mostly feel their energy as one unit of energy. I feel their embodiment and eternal power and wisdom. It is not possible to describe in words the power that the sisters of the temple hold. All I can tell you is that we are all united. I feel like they are a part of me, and I am a part of them, especially since I have been completely and fully initiated into the temple. It took me two years to be initiated myself. They have told me the first time that they channeled through me and spoke to me, it will take 2 years, and it did.
(I share more about my initiation in the book *Sex Magic Evolution as* well.)
Like the stars themselves in their journey in the skies, I feel that

my journey with the temple has been in such perfect alignment.

I feel aligned more and more each day, with myself, with the world, with my mission on Earth, and with the knowledge and wisdom that have been bestowed upon me. And now it is bestowed upon you as well.

Receive it lovingly. Use it wisely.

I love you, brothers and sisters.

Let's Dive In. The overflowing waters of the mother have been waiting for us to return to her womb.

To return to the temple.

WHAT IS THE TEMPLE?

A sex temple was a place (and still *is* in the other realm) where men and women came to train in sexual art and magic. Where humans came to heal and learn about the sacred union.

Yes. It is an actual magic school.

A sex magic school and temple. (Though they have different words to describe it.)

The temple is created, run, and taught by women. Goddesses, who were themselves initiated into the temple themselves. Chosen by a higher calling, serving all life and the mother herself.

These sex priestesses devoted their lives, spirit, and bodies to this work. They knew the significance and importance of such work.

Many of the pyramids were sex temples. Not all of them, but they are usually the smaller pyramids, hidden around the world. There are remaining and symbols found from those temples, but I have been told by the sisters, that the temple-pyramids have not yet been found. Only one was found in Bosnia so far. They are THAT well-hidden from us and for a reason. Now, knowing about the power they contain, I know humans will not be able to hold the power of the temple yet, and also there cannot be a risk of humans destroying them in any way or misusing the energies in those temples. Many have tried. Dark magicians. For they know the importance and power they possess for humanity.

There is only a handful of dark magicians who actually know about the sex temple and its realm, as well as its connection to our world. I asked the sisters if writing this book won't place the temple at risk and they said that humans need to know of the temple and learn from it now. It will be the path of highest awakening at this timeline on the planet, and because those who will do the work of the temple, though there are only a few of them capable of actually doing it, the temple will be safe within their energy field. They, in fact, will become a sort of guardians for the realm of the temple by their courage, honesty, and commitment.

When the dark masculine world destroyed and hid the temples and killed many of the sex priestesses, they took away most of the human power. The time of sleep has begun.
Humans began to have disconnected sex, which disconnected them very fast from themselves and each other and wars began to spread like wildfire. A world without the sex temple was a breeding ground for low-frequency entities to enter rapidly.

Sex was the primer way to connect to source and receive spiritual enlightenment, as well as physical healing and rejuvenation- but ONLY WHEN DONE CORRECTLY.
Sex holds so much power that the knowledge of its secrets and

potential had to be kept in the right hands. Unfortunately, when the dark masculine energy began to take hold and men came with weapons and hate and anger to take and pillage and destroy, many priestesses had to flee and a few managed to hide the temple with the help of the surrounding villagers and initiates as well as what we call- magic. They somehow transported themselves and the temple into another dimension where it was kept safe until now, but these temples, and sisters- are very much still connected to our realm.

The sex temple-pyramids are highly sacred and important. Therefore, no man can find them.

WALKING THROUGH THE TEMPLE

The temple is a place to worship the goddess and god. Sacred geometry was placed everywhere to create and attract specific energy. The different chambers and symbols created vortexes and held an energy that symbolizes and imitates the womb energy.

The temple was a place to make offerings. A place for cleansing, healing. A place for ceremonies, celebrations, childbirth and creation, nature worship, and connection. It was a sacred, safe space where the priestesses were summoning (as well as banishing when needed) energy through sex.

They had a temple for worship and schools. Mystery schools, where humans learned about the mother. The mother has always been a mystery. Her entire existence an endless riddle and a quest. A quest that leads one to their own inner 'womb'.

They used fire and water a lot in the rituals as well as oils, aromatherapy, flowers, candles, and singing. (Religion had demonized the feminine voice as well because it is extremely powerful and enchanting.)

The temple ceremonies focused on sexual energy and sexual healing. That does not mean that there was always actual penetration! The priestesses *lived* this sexual energy. It is more than just the act of sex as we view it today. Today we hold such a narrow, limited understanding of what sex is.

There are many levels of sex. It can take many forms and take you to different dimensions. It all depends on what energy you put into it. What portal you are opening.

(Learn more about this knowledge in – *Sex Magic Evolution*)

The goddess takes you to heaven. That is the energy she brings. She connects you and elevates your spirit. She is healing, sensuality, motherhood, love. She brings awakening, not just a blow-job or a fuck- the way women are viewed today when it comes to their worth and sex is highly disturbing from a perspective of a temple priestess. Most of us have gone too astray from our divine sexual power.

THE TEMPLE SISTERS

The women were chosen or had a deep calling to serve the temple. Some of them even had special gifts and powers.

High priestess (ISIS) is the embodiment of the goddess herself. The mother. She was and still is, highly respected. There was no 'leader' in the temple, for all priestesses worked together, but if there was- ISIS would have been her.

Today, we have men priests who rape children- we have turned such a sacred divine life and role of the feminine, into a dark, demonic mass ritual, with the dark religion of men. But the priestess of the temple would inspire the men to have a psychedelic experience. They often fell asleep while the priestess invoked dreams and lucid dreaming upon their energy body.

The priestesses and initiates would dance for the man, entrancing the man with their bodies and voices, challenging in a way, and provoking his shadow as well as light in order to heal, transform his energy and move his sexual energy correctly. This dance, by the way, is where the modern women stage show came from. It is done today in many forms, from belly dance performance in a community celebration, to a lap dance in a strip club. It is a natural ability the woman has, but unfortunately, women today have lost the wisdom that comes with it. The temple's sacred dance turned into a lap dance today but has no more of the sacredness and wisdom or knowledge left in it. let along with love. The women today perform the sacred dance, but it is naked from all its sacredness. This shows us though, that this temple work is ingrained in our psyche and there will always be a need for it. I pray we will add the power back into it. We can change the world if we do.

The priestesses would see the men they danced to or healed, as a god. They knew how to invoke the GOD out of this man. Many men would cry often or have breakdowns and breakthroughs in the temple. Many could not bear it and walked away, but something in them would be forever changed, nonetheless.

In the temple, the priestess chooses the man, and she takes him to another space alone if he is ready. The priestess leads the ritual (whatever ritual is needed) and he trusts her and gives the temple a gift, an offering- as well as to the earth itself.

The man often had to serve the priestess first and if he was worthy, she would serve his sexual power as well. If he isn't, she will usually teach him how to be a better lover and use his sexual energy correctly and send him away to practice and prepare himself for the next time.

Prostitution was a spiritual practice before. Though it was far from the way prostitution is used today. Sex was used to heal men and heal the world. The temple knows the connection we all have with all existence and that the power of sex is what creates the waves and webs that connect all.

You, dear masculine, must be chosen by the priestess. She will allow only men who are worthy of her energy.

Sex with a priestess is having sex with the goddess herself.

Uniting with source.

THE RETURN OF THE TEMPLE

Many humans are incarnating right now. Many are dying in their lifetimes and are re-birthed while still in the same body. They have the same memories of this life, but they are re-birthing themselves into a different version of themselves. This is confusing, I know. Many feel the death of an old life in every way, and they incarnate again, without ceasing to be in the same physical body. If you are reading this book, you are most likely one of those people.

The knowledge of the temple will come from the womb and rise into the heart and from there, after a time of heart-opening, will then rise to the third eye and only when knowledge is truly known and received in the purest way, it will be spoken- through the throat chakra.

The priestesses of the temple must unite with the gods of the temple as often as possible. They must learn the initiation. They must learn exactly how to invoke ISIS and Lilith and have them present in the union. You, together with ISIS and LILITH, form the sacred 3. Which is what the God in the man needs to awaken. (You can learn more about the exact sex priestess routine and initiation in–T*he Sex priestess manual.)*

This is the most crucial time for mankind, and women are the ones who will bridge the new and old. Mostly they will be sex priestess, whether or not they are aware of this title. Many women naturally remember who they are and are beginning to embody the memories and gifts of the priestess.

CONNECTION TO THE TEMPLE

Self-mastery takes time, dedication, and commitment. Above all, it takes maturity and a strong, honest sense of responsibility.

We all need to grow up. Now. So that we can connect to the realm of the temple and bring the light codes through us, our vessels, into this world in the best way possible. We must stop following other people's ideas and religions and governments. We must stop waiting for a savior and placing our faith and life in some external force- weather it is the government, aliens, mommy and daddy, or our partner. We must be a ready vessel and channel to bring and hold these frequencies that will birth the new world of the mother. WE- are the ones we have been waiting for. This is the most important message the temple wants to seed in us.

We have all heard of stories of seamen battling a sea monster or enter a cave to battle a monster. This is, of course, symbolic of semen that is entering the womb. The abyss. The portal. The realm of the goddess.

The sea-men (semen- the masculine) fear it but must enter it to retrieve a treasure of some sort- it is his connection to light. They must penetrate the darkness to discover light- as we have learned about the fears of the masculine and feminine in Level 1.

The cave represents the cervix and swallows the seamen, who try to attack it with the phallic sword – the symbolism of 'slaying the monster' refers to the overall fear of the masculine of the feminine and its desire- whether it be with good or bad intentions- to conquer her.

THE SISTERS SPEAK TO ALL HUMANITY

"As these stories began circulating, the world was being guided more and more, into a male dominant society. Stories are important, so are symbols- which stories are always filled with- so we urge those who read this book and are storytellers to flood the consciousness of humanity now with stories that show the rise of the divine feminine within the human psyche to bring that reality to the surface.

Your bibles are filled with such stories that have programmed humanity and created an enslaved society ruled by fear and shadow male power. Now, we ask you to use the knowledge and awareness you have about symbols, to begin observing with your eyes of inner wisdom, and see through the veils of lies and disinformation. To pierce the veil of illusion by understanding the endless symbolism that has been used to deter you from your power and use the symbols yourself while aligned with your true spirit. Connecting to the temple will help you see the truth and gain deeper wisdom of the use of symbols. Prepare your vessel as we have guided you in level 1 and master your sexual flow each day, with a pure and clear vessel and mind. Master your emotions, especially your fear, so it will not be used against you ever again."

"Brotherhood and Sisterhood hold an extremely valuable place within the temple. It is a natural way of life to constantly cultivate Sisterhood within the daily life of the temple between the sisters.
Brotherhood still has to be taught and mastered, but it is a more natural state within the men in our world. They live closer to the earth, even if they are not in their full divine essence. The men in our world worship the feminine in all her forms and manifestations- as women, nature itself, animals, and art. The men of our world spend more time with their brotherhood with a constant intention to hold each other accountable to live in their highest physical and spiritual state.

"The warriors among the men learn how to be guided by their hearts and when they go into battle, they do not conquer, but they battle with the focus on protection. They protect all life. We have had a few times where we needed the help of divine male warriors. These loving, brave men were there for the temple whenever we needed them. Unfortunately, they could not always help in the last days, for the dark could not be defeated with only a sword. Once the animals started being consumed and killed, the portal was open and we began to have more experiences of rape of women and stealing and fighting for egotistical reasons among the different Clans, but as soon as the rape of children began, we knew it is the end of our world as we know it.

"We knew that our world must be divided to protect the temple. So it was that through extreme high magic we have elevated the consciousness of the temple to a higher dimension where it can be safe and protected. And we have had to release the rest of our reality and allow the rest of the humans to go on and continue their path of learning, even though it was extremely difficult and painful for us to do. We could not rescue humans; we could not have done anything at that point.
That was the point of no return, if you will, for human consciousness at

that time. It needed to go through the deepest darkness, just like you are going through right now.

"Whoever is reading this book will immediately receive the light codes of the Temple and will be able to connect to the dimension where the temple still exists. We need to connect to you just as much as you need to connect to us now. Not many people will be able to connect with the temple but those who are will be able to bring forth back into your dimension new light codes of information that will help the Ascension of Your World."

GIFTS OF THE SISTERS

"We have mentioned earlier that some sisters of the temple had unique gifts. Each sister had their own unique gift, of course, but some had gifts that are beyond your human capacity to understand at this point. We can describe it as something like time travel, dimension travel, flying, creating material out of pure energy, building protection walls and different kinds of protection Magic- which is, by the way, the same abilities that allowed us to leave our world and transform into a different dimension where the temple would be safe. Other gifts were similar to what you would call seeing the future timeline, deep healing, and changing past experiences.
Some of us were extremely gifted midwife and were able to bring forth the child into the world with no pain for the mother or the child. It was a blessed wonderful experience - participating in the birth of the child.
Some sisters had wonderful capabilities with their voices, and they brought forth different and messages if you will from other dimensions. Yes, we were able to connect and communicate directly with many other dimensions."

"Many women in your world still hold these gifts in one way or another, but unfortunately this reality and Society has been blocking these gifts

from women and children that are coming with these gifts as well.

The main things that are blocking gifts from a human are: 1. Nutrition - (especially consuming animals and their by-products), 2. alcohol & highly processed foods. 3. Vaccines - man-made vaccines and pharmaceuticals are extremely harmful to human capacities to be completely expressed. And of course- 4. The use of your Sexual Energy- the way you have been using sex today in your world is extremely destructive even for young children. They are growing up feeling extremely confused about their sex, their gender and they find it challenging to express their sexuality in a healthy, divine way. It is not a safe reality for your children. And this must change.

"Humans have forgotten who they are, and we pray that with these words we will at least inspire you and plant a seed of remembering within your soul.

"You must stop using children and women as a sexual object and stop eating flesh and drinking blood. When you know, once again, how to manipulate and use this energy and invert it once more into its original form of divine flow which we hold as human beings, align your physical actions with your soul and heart- only when we use this power in a divine way, we shall Live In the Garden of Eden once more.

"The Earth shall rise to a new dimension no matter what- the question is- will you rise with it or remain stuck in this mind prison for more Cycles to come?"

DREAMING

In the temple, dreams and imagination were the main ways to time travel (as they are today, we had simply forgotten how). The sisters combined sexual energy with their imagination and could time travel as well as travel to other dimensions and realms. They foresaw the fall of the temples as well. The priestesses say they did not fight it or try to stop it. They knew it was inevitable, yet they had the knowledge and time to prepare and transfer themselves into another dimension where they were safe and kept doing their work. They are still in the temple, even at this moment, practicing and preserving the wisdom of sex magic. That is how they are speaking to me and to you. The temple is alive. It will always be alive. That is how powerful the priestesses are. That is how the power of our sex, imagination, and our dreams is. We are eternal.

Technically, we are all time travelers. We travel in time. All the time. There is only one point in time, one eternal moment. It is our perception that shifts and makes it appear to us that "time" is moving as past and future.

THE PYRAMID

The temple is a pyramid.

The pyramid itself was built from earth combined with crystals and other materials which we will not discuss at the moment because most of them are unknown to us today anyway.

The menstrual blood of the Priestess was as well concealed within the walls of the temple. Sigils and symbols were carved deep in the walls. Some seen on the outside walls, and some inside the wall itself.

The energy that was created from the rituals, sexual spells, and divine unions, created specific energy which is so powerful for the human mind to even conceive at the state it is today. You cannot find this type of energy in this specific formatting or coding of information nowhere else in the world right now.

Even today, when so much of our earthly time is passed, that energy still remains within the pyramids. Those who stand on the ground above those pyramids (the hidden ones we mean) will experience great uplifting of their spirit and physical healing. And those who are more aligned, open, and clear with their energy, can experience tremendous 'downloads' of information and spiritual awakening.

If you go to the one pyramid that has been found- in Bosnia- you can absolutely feel that energy today, though it has been diminished in a substantial way because of the chaotic energies that many humans have brought to it over the years. There have been too many visitors with very low vibration and very harmful intentions which have entered the pyramid. Some people just entered because of an innocent curiosity, but unknowingly have been distorted the energy within it. Remember, no abused animals have ever entered the temple, and no people who have consumed them, and the fact that humans enter it today with that frequency in their DNA, shift the entire space. This is just one reason how humans can harm and destroy the temple energy, so you can imagine why they all must stay hidden. But as we said, despite this 'energy chaos' if you will, that tremendous power that has been created so long ago by the Priestesses of the Temple still remains and lingers and cannot be completely destroyed.

The symbols and the blood of the priestesses carved within the walls are the main reasons for this.

They explain- 'We have made sure that this energy and wisdom will be kept alive, even in the slightest bit, in order for this information to be awakened in the right time by the right people. Those of you who have found your path to this book, have found the true knowledge of the Temple and we ask you to use it wisely and with the highest respect and commitment.'

Sex magic tip for masters:

Combine semen and sacred menstrual blood on a full moon, after a sacred sexual union, and mix it with your new house foundations. You can carve your own sigils along the walls or foundation bricks.

When you use sexual fluids for sex magic, you know now (if you read my book- *Sex Magic Evolution*- and I hope you have) that the partners must have a clean and pure vessel (body). Pure of animal products, alcohol, other partners' energy, etc... the partners need to have gone through the initiation period of their own self-preparation – body, mind, heart, and spirit. Since we have no temple and priestesses to go to today, the book *Sex Magic Evolution* guides you through your basic self-initiation period and gives you all the foundations of sex magic knowledge so you will be ready as a channel/ vessel of light and pure light coded information.

PART 2
WHAT ARE SYMBOLS?

WHAT ARE SYMBOLS?

Symbols, especially geometric symbols, hold a frequency that can awaken a human being.

They have the power to re-connect us with lost knowledge and hidden truths. The imbalance within our inner being, between our masculine and feminine energies, has been creating our reality in this dimension, instead of our divinity. Humans have been asleep and under a dark spell for too long.
Understanding the sacred symbols, which are in fact, a form of highly charged sigils, and connecting with their power once more is one of the greatest tools we have now.

The name of the goddess ISIS, for example, has been used as a symbol for evil magic.
Her energy and essence have been awakened in many women now, just as the energy of LILITH (which we will discuss later), but her image and symbol have been used and have been demonized by those of the dark masculine world.

You see, when you do magic, any magic, you want to use the most powerful symbol and you want to have the most powerful vessel to bring the magic forth into this reality. That is why women are used in satanic rituals in such horrific ways because they are the strongest vessels- they hold a womb. As well as children, who hold the power of imagination and with that power can conjure up endless realities and worlds. This use of baneful sex magic goes beyond pedophilia - it is the use of the most powerful vessels in order to give the magic the most power.

Of course, this kind of evil magic comes with a huge price for the soul. Those who practice such magic will lose their soul. Quite literally. And it happens very easily and very fast.

Women and children are the vessels to open portals to other sources/ dimensions, that is why they are being used. Just like the symbol and name of ISIS - a name that holds so much information and power- it is used to bring so much darkness. We see this, of course, in the use of the name for the terrorist groups - named after the goddess herself.

It is important we begin to understand and master the use of symbols. The world is in such chaos, mostly because of symbols and magic that have been used against us, while harnessing our life force.

Many have been trying to awaken humans with the truth of these hidden symbols for a long time. in this book we will explore the knowledge from the temple itself and in particular, the temple of ISIS and LILITH.

The sisters explain that many temples have been awakening once more through certain humans at this time, in the last few years, but the archetype of Lilith and the wisdom of ISIS is particularly connected and needed in our world at this time and that is why they are sharing this knowledge at this point.
We are intertwined in our destiny – both our world and the dimension of the temple- and that is why they have been reaching out, seeking a way to enter the consciousness of mankind once more.

THE MAGIC OF SYMBOLS

A symbol is in fact a Sigil.
A sigil is a specific, intentional created *form*. A symbolic shape of specific energy, information, or desire.

Symbols are all around us. Every corporation has a logo. Every logo is a sigil. A powerful symbol created to 'trap' your attention and in many cases- program your subconscious mind. Have you ever wondered about the term: 'corporate ENTITY? Now, that you know a bit more about magic and use of words and spells (as we mentioned in level 1) can you see what these words actually mean? It is shocking, I know. So, every corporation has an *entity*. A spirit that they worship, and that gives them power and success in return. (of course, this is an illusion of success since those who feed this entity knowingly lose their souls.) The employees of a corporation, unknowingly give their power and life force and time to this entity. Feeding that energy with their work, time and energy. That is why logos are so important and are always used. You will find no company with no logo.
I am not corporation, but even I use logos- several of them, which I charged with the power of the temple and with specific intentions to help humans awake to their true power- which is one of my missions and the focus of my work. Corporations usually use high baneful magic.

Governments and Hollywood use symbols. Gangs as well as secret societies use symbols to influence and connect you with the energy and realm they wish to create. They use symbols to manipulate our subconscious mind, but once we have the knowledge of symbols- we cannot be controlled any longer. Once we are conscious and aware- we become the masters of our subconscious mind as well.

In the sex temple, symbols have been used in the everyday life of the priestesses, as well as in the highest rituals.

These powerful symbols were not called sigils of course. In the sex temple of Isis and Lilith, they had a specific word for sigils, which I am not allowed to reveal at the moment (The priestesses of the temple tell me it is not important- they will not even tell me what it is. I learned to trust them at this point) and understanding the energy and the usage of the symbols is far more important right now for those who wish to awaken to their divine powers and use the sacred symbols in the best way they can today in the modern world.

There are specific magical symbols that human beings are using every day without knowing. We call them numbers.

Numbers are in fact, extremely powerful magical symbols. They are codes that hold specific frequencies and information within them. Numbers are symbols which hold specific energy and information. Numbers have been used in the temple in specific ways which we will be discussing later. The priestesses are going to reveal the most powerful secrets of the most sacred symbols on this planet.

Are you ready?

Because once you dive into the knowledge of the Temple, your subconscious is transformed and there is no turning back.

HOW TO WORK WITH THE SYMBOLS?

When working with the symbols of the temple, you first look at the symbol with your physical eyes, then you use another eye - your third eye - to look inward and feel and see the experience that the symbol creates in your body.

What does it provoke in you?

Where in your body do you feel it?

Do you see any colors or shapes?

Do you have any memories or feelings coming up?

It can be very subtle, so take the time to observe your physical vessel (your body) as well as your emotions when you observe the symbol. Seek with every eye that you have. Listen with your eyes as well. Listen and observe with your womb (or heart if you are a man). Be focused and present, but also relax and let go of your mind and any past expectations or stories or ideas about the symbol. Forget even what is written in this book for just a moment... a symbol might just reveal specific secrets that are meant just for you...

Because symbols have more than one meaning, they carry a lot of information within them. Use the symbols that your soul calls you to use as often as you can. This will activate the light codes and information that YOU need to receive at this moment.

We must become very present observers of this reality. We must see and feel deeper into the external symbols that surround us. Notice what shapes and symbols repeat in your reality. What symbols or shapes make you feel a certain way.

A good way to re-program your mind is to stop doing what you always do: take a different path to work, use calmer voice when you usually want to yell, stop and give money to that homeless you always just pass by. Once you begin changing your behavior in your reality, especially when you 'surprise' yourself with a different action, you 'shake up' your reality and you can notice this matrix better.

Use the information from this book but feel from your womb or your heart (whether you are a feminine or masculine being) to choose what symbol to use right now in your life and how to use it. The symbol itself will tell you.

The symbols are living entities.

Respect and make sure your intentions are pure to work with these symbols. Especially if you wish to connect with the temple itself and receive the true information and light codes from it.

The symbols your connection to the temple, if used correctly. Use them with respect, wisdom, and love.

You may place a symbol on your altar. You may put it as a screensaver on your phone. You may draw it at any time you wish to connect with it.

Look at the symbol and focus on it for as long as you can and remain open, let go of the mind and expectations, and ask the symbol to receive the information from it and the power that it holds. This is not a conscious practice. It is completely empowered by the subconscious mind.

Let go of any thought. The energy of the symbol will usually come in a subconscious way to the initiate. You may feel specific energy, the cells of your body might change, you may receive information in dreamtime, or in a form of pure inspiration and knowledge. You may feel an elevation of your emotions or overall energy, tingling in your body or even an enhanced sexual stimulation.

Working with the symbols in the right way, as taught by the

temple will help your etheric body and your spirit to transport into a parallel timeline for you to be aligned with the path best for you that has already been created in the ether. It will help you align yourself with your highest manifestation. You are basically aligning yourself with your true self and your true timeline and the life that you want to live. This is a pure manifestation through the powers of the temple's sex magic secrets.

"Seek and ye shalt find" -matt. 7:7

HIDDEN IN PLAIN SIGHT

Here we have the 'power' symbol.

We all use and see it with our eyes daily but most of us don't understand the true meaning of the hidden secret it holds.

A 'hidden in plain sight', basic knowledge of sexual union:
The masculine within the feminine= power= life.

This symbol literally shows the masculine force (the vertical line), penetrating the feminine body (the vessel, the chalice. The womb). And when that happens there is a creation of life- power. Interesting, no?

Now, let us begin the exploration of the sacred sex magic symbols. We all know these, but now, we shall truly KNOW and see the truth they hold. Allow the words in this book to be a mere doorway and use your own imagination and inner guidance system to reveal more wisdom from these symbols. Perhaps you will discover knowledge that cannot be written but only felt.
You have all the wisdom within you.

Here is another example: Symbols of Love.

The most well-known symbols of love in our society are surely the heart, as well as the marriage rings which couples gift each other when they promise to stand together throughout their lives.
In Chinese philosophy, this emotion is also symbolized through the sign of the Yin and Yang — a perfect circle of light and darkness complementing each other; a sign of the male and female energy. It is a perfect representation of the 4 polarities (which I hope you have mastered by now with the first level of sex magic in the book: *Sex Magic Evolution*). This symbol was not used in the temple itself and came long after the last temple was gone, but it is a great symbol to use to program the mind to unite all 4 polarities: The light and shadow of the masculine and feminine.

"Far more powerful than religion, far more powerful than money, or even land or violence, are symbols. Symbols are stories. Symbols are pictures, or items, or ideas that represent something else. Human beings attach such meaning and importance to symbols that they can inspire hope, stand in for gods, or convince someone that he or she is dying.
These symbols are everywhere around you."
—Lia Habell, Dearly, Departed

PART 3
THE SACRED SYMBOLS

"Symbolism is the language of the mysteries. By symbols men have ever sought to communicate to each other those thoughts which transcend the limitations of language"

- Manly Hall

THE CIRCLE

The most known and potent symbol used in the occult is the circle. Many people use the circle for protection during their magic, however, the power that the circle holds is much more than that.

The Circle represents the division between one space and another by using the most efficient means possible.
It is known to many that the circle represents Saturn and the cycles of nature but the real reason that you should always do your magic, including sex magic of course, within a circle is that it represents, in its purest form- **God!**
The Book of Revelation says: " I am the Alpha and the Omega. The first and the last. The beginning and the end".

The circle is the zero-field point of manifestation and connection to all realities, space, and time. To all possibilities. Within it, you are creating and forming your own world. You become a universe within a universe. You are the creator of your world, the

observer, a sovereign being, connected to endless realms. You go within. You do not follow any other idea, man, religion, story within the circle. You write your own.
You are all and nothing. The beginning and the end.

All information and knowledge, all existence, in between the beginning and the end, is encoded in the symbolism of the circle.
In a circle, you can pick any spot to start from and that exact spot will be the ending as well.

In our timeline and society, the Circle is wholeness. Unity and infinity within its naturally created focus. It is the womb. The eternal space where all life is created within. It is nurturing, protective, and perfect in its completion.
It symbolizes as well- Revolution, centering, and initiation. Circles bring awareness and focus to what is *in* them, and a sense of completion to the energy it holds.

To the Celtics, circles were used as a symbol of time, and the changing seasons. It represented and held within it the power of nature itself, as well as used to draw, of course, protective boundaries.
The Chinese saw the circle as a symbol for the heavens. The Chinese art depicting a square within a circle symbolizes the union between heaven and earth. And as I see this symbol- A Whole balancing union of two- Form and structure within the eternal cosmos. Masculine within the feminine. Order within the chaos.

The first circles mankind has seen were the sun and moon. We saw them with our eyes, the irises, and pupils which are microcosms of the universe itself. Round and perfect, unique, and enchanting. We know today by the science of Iridology that all that is happening in one's body can be seen in the irises, a complete mirror of the cosmos and ourselves.

Our ancestors have observed the movement of the seasons and cycles of life looking up to the sky to the changing heavenly bodies. A movement that was seen as what it really is perhaps- magical alchemy of life itself.

The circle will enhance and bring focus to whatever is in its center. This is something we all understand naturally, even as children, as we draw our circles in the sand. It calms the subconscious mind, creates a kind of 'home', a 'shelter' to our psyche and energy.

To many Native American tribes, the circle symbolizes the sun, the moon, energy itself, life cycles, the womb. The symbol of the Medicine Wheel and the Four Directions is a famous one for most people today.

The circle in a way unites man and spirit. Man and God. Therefore, the subconscious power that it creates on the psyche when performing magic, giving the subconscious mind the authority of God.

Wheels, planets and their rotation, clock, rings, portals... all have one thing in common- the circle that forms them. Ruled by time, yet eternally timeless. Held within the round borders yet holds all freedom and infinite energy and potential. This is the power, the mystery, and the gift of the circle.

HOW TO DRAW THE MAGICIAN'S CIRCLE

You are creating a safe space for your magic. An imaginary

boundary between you and any realms you do not wish to connect to. Between your own world and any other.

It requires focused visualization and use of your imagination and emotion = the conscious and subconscious working as one, as needed for any magic (we have mastered this in book 1- *Sex Magic Evolution*).

Invite the white-golden light to draw your circle and envelope your body. This light is created from within you. It is the only light you need to ever use in a circle and in most of your magic. Do not follow other dark magicians any longer. You create your own path. And it is guided by your highest soul. Stay away from other's spells, invocations, or sigils. Make your own. Prepare your vessel (body), as taught in book 1, and become your own God/ guide. The teachings of the temple are given to you so that you will be ready to embody the full god/ goddess on earth and birth together a better world.

Draw the circle clockwise. You can, of course, draw it physically if you wish with salt, earth, sacred blood (as opposed to blood taken by force which is extreme baneful magic and should never be used), but it is best you use your imagination and practice strengthening your MIND so that the circle will be around you most of the day, even when not performing magic. Get to the point where magic *becomes* you. Where your every moment in life IS magic. IS connected and guided by your own soul's power.

This practice will also program your mind to know your connection and alignment to ALL life. All beings, realms, and will align you with your heart. Just imagine if we had many humans in this state of consciousness walking among us every day... just imagine the world we can live in.

Many suggest using a blessed dagger or sword. But I like my own hand-made wand or even just my hand. When the hand is connected to the heart and my womb, it becomes the most powerful tool. For men a sword or dagger is great or a wand of some sort, because it correlates with the masculine direct, focused energy.

Once your circle is sealed do not cross the boundary until the magic is done. All spirits are released and all portals you have opened are sealed.

PROTECTION

Always do any magic within the Sacred Circle for it represents the infinite, the nature of energy. It's meaning is universal and easy for the subconscious mind to grasp.
The circle is wholeness itself, and within it, your subconscious mind knows it has the authority of God.
The circle, combined with our power, creates a vortex where we are untouchable to evil.
We are protected.
When we draw the circle, the vortex is formed, together with our intention, our emotion and of course, our imagination.
The circle can also be drawn around any entity, energy, or thought form you feel is there to harm you in any way. Enclosing it with its own circle. You can leave that circle sealed, separate from you, and know you are safe and free from all baneful energies. At all times. You have the power to bind and banish any entity that is not in your best interest.
You have the authority and power.
But... and this is a big but! - this place of power and authority must be aligned to your heart. If guided by your ego-mind you are inviting trouble. Lower spirits are just looking for this kind of

human to bond with, to invite into a contract, a promise of giving you some information or power, only to take all you have in return. Therefore it is vital you take the time to prepare. If you haven't yet- stop now and go through the self- initiation period as suggested in book 1 (*Sex Magic Evolution*). Do not skip any step. Do not rush. You must build a strong vessel, inside and out that can hold all the light codes of the temple.

Remember you are no less and no more than any being in existence. This is the subconscious wisdom of the circle. You can, from this place, connect to all your fragmented parts, to all the versions of you in all time and space. This magic work is not to be logically understood and dissect, though the irony is that when you are ready and awaken to your inner godliness, you don't even need to understand, for you KNOW this. All makes sense and all flows to you and through you divinely.
This is why the self-initiation time and commitment is crucial.

The circle, with all its power, demands maturity and responsibility from the magician. There are no spirits higher than you or lower than you. A powerful magician knows that he/she will never bow down or give their freedom to any spirit. Therefore, you MUST ALWAYS know thyself. A God/dess always takes responsibility for themselves in every way. They do not rush, find short cuts or external power to save them. The circle demands us to be those gods and to bring forth this wisdom to the reality outside our circle.

The temple still exists right now, simultaneously, in another dimension. We must go through this human form to get there. The portal we create within the circle can not only connect us to our soul's highest path but to the temple itself and our soul's mission. We can receive the light codes better and faster once mastering the art of the circle. The simplest shape, but the most profound one for the human psyche.

Those who cannot embody and become a Magi within the circle are not ready for the light codes of the temple and will need more work of preparation with body, heart, and soul healing and purification, to charge the realm of imagination and cleanse, prepare and activate their DNA to their own life force awakening.

THE CAVE

Another symbol that is birthed from the circle is the energetic story and symbolism of a cave.

The temple itself has many caves and caverns within it. Each space designated to another priestess or ritual or even a sort of 'class' for those who came to learn about the secrets of sex magic. (The priestesses laugh at my use of word 'class' here because there is not even a word correlational to it in their language. How they call their 'classes' is something like – transformation of information.)

All bibles and many ancient stories tell of a wise man gaining enlightenment. This man usually enters a cave for a long period of time to gain this knowledge or enlightenment.

When a divine man seeks his true awakening, he must seclude himself in a 'cave', a 'man-cave'. He must remain in silent, even darkness, literally, for a long period of time, alone, until he gains enlightenment.

This cave he enters is only a preparation for the eternal cave he must face- the womb. These stories were reminders for men to always prepare and do spiritual work before entering a woman. The feminine. Before coming together in a divine union.

This is also a metaphor for a divine masculine (who respects and understands the power of the eternal wisdom of the womb), who enters the portal of life, and spends a 'long time' inside. Meaning- he does not simply go 'in and out' and ejaculate for his own pleasure. He enters, holding his selfish desires, uniting with the cave (the womb, the feminine, the mother) to gain enlightenment. A new, powerful, connection to source itself. To GOD.

This is the eternal darkness and the place that holds all life potential. He enters it with reverence, humility, takes his time, and leaves it renewed on all the levels of his being. And above all, he has created a new reality. A 'baby'. Life. He embodies, truly- God.

THE CONE OF POWER

The pulsating energy that we invoke from within the circle, is spiral-like and is known as 'the cone of power'. It is the name for this spiral energy we rise in ritual and spell work.

Many witches, including myself, have never heard of this term but have been raising a spiral energy from a circle naturally. A witch knows what to do, even if no one teaches her (or him), for we already have all the knowledge within us. It is only a matter of connecting with this knowledge. To our inner magi (= i—magi-nation).

The cone and circle are also associated with eternity and rebirth and with the symbol of the Sun. you are literally enclosed and safe within your own sun. A life creating light and warming fire.

The cone is one of the most important symbols of the temple as well. In the temple, the spiral is often seen within the diamond. You see when you stand in the circle, and your energy spirals up in a cone-like shape upwards, as well as downwards, what you get, from a side point of view- is the diamond. It is the way that the grid-work of the circle moves energetically- up and down. Male and female. Heaven and earth, and you – in the center of it, creating it. Sending the waves of energy in and out of you, simultaneously. We will learn more about the diamond later.

"A blessing is a circle of light drawn around a person to protect, heal and strengthen them."
~ *John O'Donohue*

THE CROSS

The cross is mainly known as the sun symbol in our culture. Though followers of religion may think it means something completely different, and ironically, as those who look and wear the cross most often, are in fact oblivious to the true power of the cross.

The cross as depicted in Christianity, with a longer lower line, represents the cube as well, which represents Saturn. Saturn is known as the black sun in the occult. There is much to learn about the cube and the catholic shaped cross, but in this book, we will focus on symbols of sex magic, and especially those used in the temple.

The cross used in the temple has 4 equal parts and it is mainly drawn on or within the circle.
The cross itself in sex magic teachings represents heaven and earth and the union of them both.
The point where the two lines cross symbolizes the divine union in the physical world, which affects and influences all directions, all worlds, and dimensions around. It shows us in the simplest form, how a sexual union- a divine masculine and feminine- with their shadow and light- affect all realities. How that one point of

union shoots energy to all directions, to east, west, heaven, and earth.

In the Christian cross, the lower line is connecting the orgasm, the union, directly into the earth, the physical plane, the mother's body herself. Therefore, it is particularly astonishing to learn how religion, and the church in particular, have demonized sexual union and completely destroyed the power of the divine feminine and masculine on our planet. It has stripped away all our real sexual powers from us and it's been hiding the truth from us for so long, while at the same time, placing it right in front of our faces the entire time- but giving it a different meaning- stripping away the true power of the symbol (and many other powerful symbols as well).

The masculine has a vertical energy flow, which is one that is grounding, stable, connecting between heaven and earth, while the feminine has a horizontal flow. One that moved through time and space endlessly. The man's path in this world is to elevate himself spiritually, and the woman's path is to stay closer to the ground. With a divine union, both can achieve this in the best way, for they have the support of the other. The woman, who is naturally more connected to spirit already, is supporting the man's spiritual growth with her loving presence, and the man, who is naturally more grounded, supports and helps the female stay more solid on the earth with his energy. He takes care of the earthly matter, while she naturally does the energy work that is embedded in her body. At least this is the potential of the divine energetic relationship between male and female- which our dark masculine society has demolished.

The cross depicted with a circle around it is one of the most known symbols of our society. In many cultures, it also represents the four physical elements (earth, water, air, and fire) and the four cardinal directions (north, south, east, and west). From ancient druids, tribes, to christianity, it has been used everywhere. But in fact, only very few know the actual meaning of it and where it came from.

There are whole books written on this symbol alone, so we will not go into full depth in this book, but I hope this to be a tease so you can go and seek the truth for yourself if you still feel the pull of the Christian or catholic religious story. The knowledge is out there, and my purpose is to empower you to find the truth and do the work, not feed you with a spoon. I will give you all knowledge you need to embark on a divine path that suits a sex goddess and god and hold the power of the temple of ISIS and LILITH, but you MUST do the work. (TIP- you can listen to Jordan Maxwell for more information about this and other symbols in religion).

The circle is an invitation to focus and observe what is inside of it- in this case- the cross, with the sacredness and energy it holds. This symbol is honored and revered by many today, even if they do not understand it fully, because people feel the energy from a symbol, especially such as a cross and a circle, both ancient, simple, and embedded with eons of information. Both generational and natural.

The cross within the circle is in fact an ancient symbol of the sun, but in the temple, it holds even deeper meaning. It holds a whole complete union.

The sun - which is in fact the son- 'the light of god' in Christianity- represents the qualities of a god. The cross divides the circle into 4 seasons- which are in fact- the 4 gospels- and the bible itself is a story- a story that tells about the life of the son (sun) of God.

The sun is the light of the world. The life-giving force that humans have worshiped for eons, and which has now turned into a joke we call- Christianity- a mind and consciousness prison created to manipulate and take human's powers from them.

BUT- if you are reading this book- you have begun your awakening, or even exploring deep inside the rabbit hole. You are on a path you cannot go back from, because once you see the truth, you cannot fall asleep again.

So, keep exploring....

It never ends...

In the school of ISIS and Lilith, the 4 corners represent the 4 opposing forces which, when united correctly, form a whole. The 4 corners (polarities) are:

The divine masculine, the dark masculine, the divine feminine, and the dark feminine.

All are needed. All are important to be observed, conquered, and used correctly, for if we do not conquer our own shadow- it controls us.

So, when creating the divine sexual union using this symbol, you are holding and controlling, in a way, all the polarized aspects of yourself and can form a more whole union. Within yourself and thus, with your partner. This symbol reminds us of these polarizing forces that play a role within each of us (we all have these 4 aspects in one degree or another)- and that we are the masters of our psyche, of our ego, of our light and shadow, and we are the ones to bring ourselves into perfect balance, honoring all parts of ourselves, and uniting them with love and intention.

ⅅℛⱯWIℕG ℱℋIS SYⲘℬOⳑ

You can draw this symbol and place it on your altar or even draw a bigger one and make love within it.
Say this prayer each time before the union:
"Divine feminine, divine masculine, unite within me."

Each partner says this 4 times, (you can use this symbol alone as well, of course) and then you can repeat it another 4 times together.
These powerful words are a spell to awaken and unite your soul, all fragmented aspects of you, and prepare you for an even more divine union.

TRIANGLE / PYRAMID

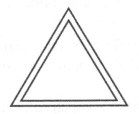

"When the mind knows itself and loves itself, there is a trinity,

a trinity of knowledge, love, and awareness."

- Lombard

In Magic, the most basic shapes are the most powerful ones. The subconscious mind might seem very complicated to us and to our conscious mind, but in fact, it works in a very simple way. Therefore, the simplest symbols have the strongest effect on the subconscious mind.

A circle is one of them, as we have discussed earlier, and a triangle is another.

It has been used in every cult, religion book in history, it has been used by witches, freemasonries, and the egyptian culture as well. At the sex magic Temple of Isis and Lilith, this symbol is not only used for almost every ritual and everyday life, but the temple itself is built within this shape- a pyramid.

The sisters have taken me to the pyramid and shown me the outside of the Temple. It is an erect pyramid- a triangle facing upwards- and underneath the ground, there is another pyramid that was built facing downwards.

The top level of the Temple, inside the erect pyramid, is where initiates live, eat, gather, and celebrate. And in the bottom pyramid is where the initiates go through their rituals, ceremonies, and highest teachings.

Together, the two pyramids create, if you haven't pictured it yet, a diamond.

In our culture, the triangle symbolizes many different meanings, and humans have been using it very often.

It represents gender (male or female- based on its position- upward or downward), power of manifestation, protection, spiritual illumination, and Ascension. It also has a shadow side from its use with dark magicians who are well known, such as celebrities and politicians. Not to mention its use by major corporations, many dark mass rituals (which we call stage shows) and wide symbolism throughout our culture.

The triangle can shift our view towards a specific way. It is the tip of an arrow, directing us to take notice and guide our focus.

A triangle is equal to the number 3- which represents the holy trinity. In religion, it is father, son, and holy spirit (which we can see has no balance with the feminine whatsoever and has taken the feminine's power- so we know it cannot be the right meaning to it).

The trinity in sex magic is- the goddess, the god- and the eternal space between and from them. The third energy they create together. It is- mother, father, child (a creation). Feminine, masculine, and source itself. All in existence. God, if you will.

In the temple, the triangle has no name, but it is simply known that this shape holds these powers.
The number 3 also represents- mind, body, and spirit. Past, present, and future (though in the temple the sense of time is meaningless.)

The triangle is used mainly for sex priestesses who are being initiated in the temple because it also represents the three pillars of the sex priestess: knowledge, wisdom & love.
This is discussed more in the Sex Priestess initiation of the sex Magic School for those who wish to become initiated priestesses.

THE POWER OF 3

Even people who have nothing to do with magic or the occult have heard the phrase: *The power of 3.* In the occult, movies, stories, and our society in general. This number and This shape have tremendous power which cannot be held captive by the dark ones. True wisdom is free and will find the hearts of the awakened ones.

In the temple, it is believed and known even, that these sacred symbols have a life of their own. Almost like a child after he/she is birthed through a human being, these symbols are forever birthed through our imagination. And we can connect to their power and empower ourselves, using them in our daily life and our sacred union.

3 represents the union itself. The union of the masculine and feminine, of numbers one and two that come before it.

It represents the 3rd dimension which we all chose to be in right now. It reminds us of our force when we come in a perfect union in the physical body. It reminds us of the worlds we can create together as we expand into a pyramid- and later into a Merkava - as we will discuss soon- with more and more dimensions added to its 3 corners.

The triangle Changes its meaning depending on what direction it is in. Unlike the circle which stays infinitely the same no matter which way you turn it.

Triangle is polarized in nature. When we understand both aspects of it and the nature of them, we can control the nature of the triangle and not be polarized by it. Depolarization is one of the biggest mastery of any initiate of the Sex Magic School and of anyone practicing magic.

ERECT TRIANGLE

Upward energy. Stability, strength balance, grounding, masculine energy, mastery, strong foundation, knowledge. Fire and air. Sun energy. Mountain. Father. Phallus.

INVERTED TRIANGLE

Downward energy. Passive, imbalance, change, danger, wisdom, mystery, female energy. Descend into the physical world. Moon energy. Cave. Womb. Mother.

Triangle reminds us to always observe ourselves and to make sure we live in complete balance within ourselves. Balance of our divine feminine and masculine together. Balance of our mind and heart. Our body and spirit. Therefore, the triangle is presented all around the temple in a form of drawings, golden amulets. It is even marked on the cave walls, and on cups and plates used for nourishment in the temple.

It reminds the initiate to uphold the structure of their commitment in their spiritual path. To each other. To remain steady and stable and grounded in their physical body while they are receiving knowledge and transmissions and light codes from the spirits of the Temple.

In the temple, every ritual was made inside the circle and its protection, while the pyramid is mostly used to focus the energy, aim it at a specific location or draw energy.

This is the knowledge that has been taught to the initiates in the higher levels of the sex Magic School.

USING THE TRIANGLE IN SEX MAGIC

The sisters of the Temple ask that this symbol will be used as frequently as possible. You may wear it in jewelry, draw on your furniture, make paintings with it, place the symbol on your altar, and focus on it while meditating.

You can find a way to place a mirror inside the triangle while you are doing mirror magic. Simply observe your reflection in the mirror for as long as you can and allow the pyramid to encase your eyes and face within it. Use the energy from the pyramid to draw energy to you or to send out energy to a beloved or the planet, whoever needs some power, or to the mother herself.

You can use the direct or inverted triangle depending on your needs and your intentions. Use the erect triangle to gain masculine focus as you work on a project or when you wish to send out energy somewhere and use the inverted triangle when you wish to receive a gift or a manifestation from the cosmos.

Enjoy the power and wisdom of the symbol to help you with your spiritual goals as well as your physical grounding and healing.

Another way to connect with your power in your sexual union is to simply draw the inverted triangle on the body of the feminine partner and draw the correct triangle on the body of the masculine partner. This is done with the intention to connect to your own divine feminine and masculine powers and to come to the union with a more Pure and Powerful body and frequency.

Once you begin to draw this symbol and play with it, it will begin to guide you in how to use it in your rituals. It will show you how it can help you and your partner's specific energies that you bring together. How it can enhance your unique gifts and love for each other. And of course- your magic.

STAR OF DAVID AND THE MERKAVA

Two worlds collide to create life. Two vortexes that come together and birth a new world.

The Merkava is also known as the star of David.

2 pyramids, each holding a dimension of their own, come together and create life in their intertwined spin and unison.
As they spin around and within each other, they create attraction and repulsion= movement. And movement is life

The symbol of the star of David has six points, six outer triangles and a six-sided hexagon in the middle. A few believe this symbol to be the 'mark of the beast'. But it couldn't be farther from the truth. During the Nazi regime, the Jews of many countries were forced to wear a yellow or white, 6-pointed star on their arm or cloths. Even children were made to wear it.
As we already know, a symbol is a sigil. It is a shape that holds within its tremendous power and information. The Jews did not

know this when they wore this symbol. But I am positive that some of the Nazi elite knew all about the sacred geometry in this shape. Even the symbol of the Nazi party itself – the swastika- was taken from Indian tradition. The swastika is a symbol of divinity in Hinduism but was reversed by the Nazis and used to spread the opposite of divinity, as we all have witnessed. Many dark magicians use sacred symbols in reverse, to harness their power to their own agenda.

Revelation:13:16
And he causeth all, both small and great, rich and poor, free and bond, to receive a mark in their right hand, or in their foreheads:
And that no man might buy or sell, save he that had the mark, or the name of the beast, or the number of his name.
Here is wisdom. Let him that hath understanding count the number of the beast: for it is the number of a man, and his number is Six hundred threescore and six.

So - is the star of David the mark of the beast?
The original name of this symbol was the 'seal of Solomon.' It was believed to be a ring that God himself gave Solomon with this symbol from heaven and that it possesses magical powers.
The star of David is a 6-pointed star- The main symbol in the Jewish tradition which only became a symbol of Judaism in the Middle Ages. Before that, the main symbol in this religion has been the Menorah: A 7 (as well as 9) branched candelabra.
A lampstand made of gold, used in the temple. It has been a reminder for the nation of Israel to be "a light unto the nations." and the prophet Zachariah had a vision explaining that this light is to be used with an intention of peace.
This seal- known as the seal of Solomon- originated in Jewish tradition but can be found as well in later Islamic and other Western branches of belief, which, in fact, have created many of

their teachings from the Jewish tradition.

Solomon had many wives, but his first wife, the daughter of Pharaoh (the king of Egypt) was given her own palace. The sisters of the temple had told me that this woman was a student of the temple. She had taught Solomon all the secrets of sex magic. He had promised her to respect and honor the power he had awakened but lied and continued to use unholy sex with his other wives. The bible says he had almost 1000 wives, but according to the sisters of the temple he had about 72 women in his palace, and he has slept and even raped a few others. The daughter of the pharaoh wasn't really the daughter of pharaoh like the bible wants us to believe, but a woman from Egypt who Solomon had taken to be his wife, knowing she will teach him the powerful knowledge. He lied to her, but she loved him. She even left the temple to be with him, thinking she can help the people if the king himself will know how to use the secrets of sex magic. She wanted to create a better world for herself and the people in her country and the lands all around. The king had told the lie that she was a king's daughter to appear more powerful to his people and to not seem weak, listening, and learning from a simple woman.

He seduced her and manipulated her, and she believed his beautiful promises only to later see who he truly is. Solomon had used the sex magic knowledge in baneful ways and with the symbol he had taken from her- not from God- he has led a whole nation into believing he was such a powerful being. This sister was the one who gave him and taught him about this symbol- what he named 'the seal of Solomon' and what later has been known as 'the star of David'.

This was one of the most important sex magic symbols used in the temple. And now, the truth is free at last, and the power of the sacred symbols returns home.

Today, this symbol is still used by many pagans, witches, and cults to summon demons. ISIS explains to me that Solomon had seeded this divine symbol with dark, baneful intention, which, we can all see the effects that are still held by humans today. We must change and transform the power of this divine symbol to what it originally was.

The Mishna (a written collection of the Jewish oral traditions) tells us that Solomon's ring had the name of God on it. The seal of Solomon was believed to be a sort of a protective shield from unwanted spirits, as well as a symbol that holds the power to divert their direction elsewhere.

It was believed that the ring could command demons, draw them into the symbol, bind them, and re-directing their energy, protecting humans from them. Jinn (genie)- an ancient name for demons from the middle east- were believed to be able to be controlled by the ring. Solomon the king placed them under his control and even questioned them of who they were, where they come from, and their intentions. The ring helped the king learn about their purpose and powers and in return, how to destroy them as well. This is all knowledge of the temple that was given to Solomon. This symbol was used for protection and summoning higher spirits for the sake of helping the world in highest intentions, through divine sexual union. But- the king reversed the power and found a way to use it for his own baneful intentions. No history book will tell you this.

It was told that Solomon the king even ordered the demons to help him build the temple and that he trapped them in bottles- which he had buried under the temple itself, once the temple was ready. (This story, of course, inspired a later tale from the book - *one thousand and one Arabian nights*)

The temple Solomon tried to build wasn't a sex temple, though he tried to imitate the sex temples with the geometry and their power. But he was not able to gain that knowledge. His temple later was destroyed. A reminder that all baneful magic never lasts.

In the sex magic school of ISIS and LILITH, this symbol represents the harmonious union of two worlds.
It is used in the higher levels of sex magic, within the masters of the temple.
It is only when you reach the level of sexual union with a god of the temple- when you can use this symbol.
It is a symbol of balance, the harmony of polar opposites, union in a polarized world, and above all- divine creation.

One pyramid points to the heavens, and the other to the earth: "as above, so below".

It creates and forms a 3rd space created in between the two, bringing protection during the union, harmony, and pure oneness.
The downward triangle/ pyramid- is the embodiment of the feminine energy, and the upward triangle/ pyramid- is the embodiment of the masculine energy.
The penis and the vulva intertwining in perfect alignment, forming a third shape between them (the hexagram). This explains why pagans have used this symbol as a sex & fertility power symbol.
This star, therefore, above all, represents creation. Union of divine masculine and feminine, and I believe this is the main reason why many cults and religions have been using it for darkness and control- because IT IS THAT POWERFUL, they have craved to harness the power within it (and many other

sacred symbols) to control humans just as Solomon was believed to control demons.

The elites have been using this symbol for too long, with a very dark, baneful intention and it has gained tremendous power while hiding the true knowledge from us.

So, what if we use it ourselves, more often, in the correct, divine way, with the true knowledge of sex magic- and change the course of the destiny in the world. What if we can create our own world, based on love, unity, truth, and freedom?

NOTE: Solomon is just a name. The sisters of the temple explain to me that the name of the man who did this dark magic was named differently in their reality, but they do not wish to speak his name at all because the powers he had created, as well as his essence, is well to be forgotten.

THE DIVINE CHARIOT

The star of David, or Seal of Solomon forms another powerful shape. When expended into a 3-dimensional shape, with 2 pyramids instead of 2 triangles- it creates a star tetrahedron.

This symbol is also called -Star Tetrahedron- in Hebrew, it is called MERKAVA- which literally translates to- the chariot of God. Or- chariot to God.

The Merkava is a vehicle of light. It is the manifestation of a new world, through a chariot. A chariot to another world.

It is used for inter-dimensional travel, either while awake or asleep. That is why it is called a chariot. It is a light vehicle for the energy body (or KA- as known in Egypt).

LIGHT AND SHADOW

like any symbol, and really, like anything in our world, there exists polarity.

A light and a shadow. We now know that the shadow was embedded by Solomon king himself to this sacred symbol, but this is true for any symbol. Any symbol has both light and dark potential within this 3rd-dimensional reality. What force you will evoke, and use depends fully on your (the magician) intention and emotions that arise looking and working with the symbol.

A symbol is a tool. It can be used for the creation of light or dark. Chronos, and other gods who represent Saturn in our culture, were depicted as eating children with this symbol connected to them so we see how a symbol can be used to both light and shadow.

The hexagram is also known as the star of Moloch. A Canaanite god who is associated with child sacrifice. Today, many worship Moloch still, unaware, thus, allowing evil forces to use their own life force. Many secret societies today are still worshiping these ancient gods, sacrificing children, and the sexual energy of children to them.

This symbol can be found openly in Luciferian and pagan locations, masonic lodges, churches, and synagogues all around the world and most humans have no idea what it means, subconsciously allowing the dark magic to work on them and suck away their life force.

Religion today is nothing more than a powerful evil spell. Energetic vampirism. It was created in a systematic, genius way for centuries, but now it is time to wake up to the hidden world of symbols that surrounds us and controlling us, through our subconscious mind, manipulating out psych and hurting our children.

This symbol has penetrated and has been used by all major religions, therefore I have no doubt it is used for baneful, evil purposes. Judaism, Islam, Catholicism, Hinduism, and many more, but this is precisely what makes this symbol powerful. The more a symbol is used for shadow, we know how it has the same amount of potential for light.

We have the power to use this symbol as well, as it was first used in the temple. We can use it with a pure, new, loving way and re-direct its power, with focused intentions, to change the reality around us, as well as our personal life.

When we learn this and are aware of these symbols, all their meanings & powers, and know how to use them better- we can shift the energies. We can literally create a new reality.

We can use the same symbols, but with an intention of love and light, and destroy the dark powers that are using the same symbols for baneful purposes against us.

This symbol can be used for extreme protection and divine union. This symbol is one of harmony and union of 2 worlds, 2 dimensions, that create a new one. A better one.

The chariot of light brings to form the unity of both polarities, masculine and feminine, light, and dark, spirit and matter, earth and heaven, and forms another world, a dimension of its own if you will.

When using sex magic energy correctly and ONLY after learning the secrets and knowledge of sex magic, you can use this symbol to carry you into another realm. This is powerful and can be dangerous. That is why this knowledge was taught in the temple only to those who have completed their initiation, which can vary in time periods, depending on the individual. (To know more about the initiation read my book: *Sex Magic Evolution*).

Once you have taken the time to connect to your soul, your own power, and understand the knowledge deeper, you are ready for the chariot, for the travel and flight of the KA, the energy body.

Another occult practice of sex magic is sex with deities, angels or even demons. I will never teach or recommend having sex with demons, and in my school, you can learn about sexual union with deities, but according to the temple of ISIS, the Merkava WILL protect you when you evoke high spirits to unite with them in sex.

Religion has painted the picture for us that the masculine is in the sky in the form of a father God. But in fact, if we look at ancient symbolism like the goddess newt (nut) which symbolized the sky, we can find the true place of the goddess and the god.
The goddess is in heaven and the God is on Earth.

The dark masculine world has used this image of a sky god, a Heavenly Father, to take the power away from the feminine and steer us away from her true nature.
This is why the downward-pointing triangle represents the feminine. She's in the sky and in heaven. Representing the spiritual eternal, ever-changing world, and her energy always moves downwards towards the physical Earth, seeking to unite with the masculine and with her children.
And the masculine is represented by the upright pointing triangle. He holds the power of the physical world, grounded and stable in his pure divine form, always seeking to move upwards and to reunite with the divine feminine, and with the spiritual world that she is the master of and offers to him.
That is why the practice of a divine woman is to find more stability, ground herself in the physical world and connect to her body, while the divine practice for a man is to reach the highest levels of spiritual potential. Both are seeking and moving towards

the opposite to create a Divine Union of both worlds within themselves.

Without this polarized movement towards each other, without this electricity and attraction of the feminine and masculine, of heaven and Earth- there is no life

And, there is no power and connection to our true nature as human beings.

This is important in learning sex Magic and how these polarities move together.

USING THE MERKAVA / STAR IN SEX MAGIC

Though many people know about the use of the Merkava today in magic, my sisters of the Temple ordered me to not teach this powerful symbol's use in Sex Magic to just anyone. This very simple yet powerful method is meant only for those who have been initiates into the temple. Only those who have been initiated and prepared. Those who have cleansed their body, mind, heart and soul will be able to fully practice this method within the energetic codes of the sex magic Temple of Isis and Lilith.

One of the reasons which I am sharing the knowledge of the Merkava in this book is because humans need to know the tools they can use. The truth has been hidden from us for too long. Although using the Merkava is a very simple method of magic to use with your imagination, it is extremely dangerous for those who are not ready and those who are not in the right frequency for it. This is why so many have been able to manipulate this symbol to the shadow instead of the light. I wish to bring back the knowledge of the temple as it should be, and I know humans need some time to prepare and respect this knowledge first.

Most people who will attempt to use this symbol with no knowledge how to do it properly, might not feel anything out of the ordinary in their everyday life, but they will create tremendous amounts of energy around them. They will also potentially cause tremendous chaos, unknowingly, in the universe, if they are not ready to use such powers. If they have not had the complete period of self- initiation and their vessel- physical and energetic body is not ready for such work.

This symbol is meant only for initiates of a specific frequency and knowledge within the temple. You may still use it if you wish like many others, yet ISIS and Lilith wish to inform you that you will be taking on a tremendous amount of risk and karma if you do not use it in the right way.

This symbol will call you when you are ready for it. It is quite a unique symbol in the temple. An entity on its own almost. This is no force to mess around with. There should be no ego, no desire for self when using it. Your body must be completely clean from any substances, animal products- which contain the lowest vibration material on this planet. You must be pure in your heart with no trauma holding you back, and you must be completely dedicated to the temple itself. Now you can see and understand why this symbol can be used only by a few- you can understand, I hope, but you must have complete dedication and be fully aligned with your soul to reach these levels. I hope that if you choose to work with these levels, in this specific Temple, you will honor yourself and the knowledge and the divine sisters who are sharing it with us now.

Remember, it is time for maturity, responsibility, and respect. It is time to awaken the God / Goddess inside of you. And this is how Gods live.

Not following these 'instructions' may cause very unwanted

karma for your own cycle of evolution. This is a warning spoken with love, but it is a warning, nonetheless.

You may choose to still live as you always have, with no magic symbols or sacred union, and take no extra responsibility on your already heavy shoulders. That is perfectly fine, and it is also understandable. But if you are reading these words, most likely you want more of life. And you want more of yourself.

We love you and we know that if you are reading this you are most likely are able to be aware of yourself and are able, to be honest with yourself about your current path and energetic state. We trust you that you choose wisely.

THE CHALICE

The inverted triangle also represents another sacred symbol. The chalice. It is also known to many in our timeline as – the holy grail.

The chalice symbolizes the womb. The womb, of course, contains the waters of the goddess.
The sacred water. The water that forms and holds life itself. The water of life, but also of pleasure. We learned about these sacred waters in book 1- the amazing liquid called Amrita.
The womb itself IS the divine chalice, pouring its heavenly waters down into the Earth. As well as on to the masculine phallus, who penetrates the womb with power and love, releasing the divine waters unto itself and the world.

Yet again we see that demonization and the reverse meaning that the dark the world has given a sacred symbol. We see this everywhere in our society. For ages.
There are many artistic depictions of a chalice and its use of holding sacrificial blood of innocents. Especially of children and

animals and it is used in all major religions. Yet the true meaning of a chalice and the temple could not be further than that.

The Chalice symbolizes the womb, and the eternal ever-flowing waters end sacred blood that is given freely from the womb.
Given out of the creation of life or pleasure and deep feminine surrendering. (See: Amrita- *Sex Magic Evolution* book)
It represents, houses, and contains these sacred fluids for the use in the temple and in divine rituals and ceremonies.
This goblet has found different meanings in Christianity and other religions throughout history. It has been used as a vessel for blood mostly. For sacrificial blood. Sacrificial blood is blood taken by force, by pain or torture from an innocent. This kind of act will never be tolerated in the temple or from anyone who wishes to enter the temple. This intention is pure evil and baneful and has nothing to do with divine sacred union or the temple itself.

The Chalice represents an abundance of life and creation.
Abundance which all humans share and have if they choose to live in harmony within their true powers and enter the temple with honor and love.
The only use of this symbol that has been closest to its true meaning, has been used by witches as a symbol of the goddess and the womb. Those who have been practicing divine magic have been using this symbol as a female element tool of initiation, in their prayers or rituals, and those have done so have been blessed by the goddess herself, whether they know it or not.
Even today the church has been practicing dark rituals in front of the eyes of millions of people that are completely unaware of the meaning behind the ritual. The pope himself and others of the church have been using the chalice and other symbols to empower their dark rituals, while using the power of the masses

and their emotions to charge their magic.

The masses of people who participate in the ceremonies of the church are in fact participating in extremely dark magic rituals that are using their own power and 'sucking' away the people's life force while using sacred symbols to open portals for lower frequency, energy, and entities.

In Christianity, The Chalice is a symbol of the holy communion and the sacrificial blood of Jesus who was crucified on the cross.

"Then he took the cup, gave thanks and offered it to them, saying, "Drink from it, all of you.
This is my blood of the covenant, which is poured out for many for the forgiveness of sins.
I tell you, I will not drink of this fruit of the vine from now on until that day when I drink it anew with you in my Father's kingdom." - Matt. 26:27

It is a symbol that has been transformed into a dark magic power symbol and has been completely forgotten and stripped away from its true meaning- the ever-flowing blood of the divine feminine that is given freely with love, not suffering, to all mankind.

The blood of life, not death and pain.

(You can learn more about the menstrual blood in book 1).

The Chalice has also been depicted many times in the art of the Christian religion, especially those depict John the Evangelist-with a serpent (Another extremely important sex Magic symbol which we will be discussing later).

There are many different meanings to this symbol within the religious world but that has no meaning to us now, as we dive deeper into the wisdom of the temple. Therefore, we will not even discuss it here. What I would like to point out is that this is another example of how the church has been using symbols and reversing their meaning and power in order to control mankind and take away their life force instead of using them in the divine way of giving life force and power to the user.

USING THIS SYMBOL IN SEX MAGIC

You can use this symbol in your sexual union as a physical chalice that you keep on your altar. Cleanse and bless it before you use it like any other tool of magic.

You can fill the Chalice with menstrual blood and drink from it or give it to the Earth as an offering and a divine sacrifice. One drop is enough, mixed with water or natural juice, but the more you can handle drinking it, the better, and the more you give to the earth the better.

You can use your regular blood in the magic as well as the masculine partner, but do not cut yourself or hurt yourself. You need only use one drop with blood magic, therefore a prick on the tip of the finger is enough.

You may take a drop from each partner and mix them together in the cup with clean water. And if you want to have an extremely powerful ritual add the sacred waters from the feminine body, by awakening the Isis River, which we will mention again later.

We call these sacred feminine water- the Amrita- squirting.

NOTE: if you can make your own chalice, it would be best. Create it out of any natural substance such as clay and water, do it on the new or full moon. Carve your name or your personal sigil into it and you can even add some of your menstrual blood into the carvings before it dries. If you are male, you can ask your beloved to use her blood or simply use a drop of your own blood. If you are in a committed union- create a chalice together. Work with divine moon time (the new moon is best for a new creation) and lay it in the sun to dry to soak up and be filled with the light of life as well.

⍟RINKING SEMEN

The sisters of the temple asked the men to drink their own semen. Yes. You read it correctly.

This way, the men could feel into the DNA structure of their own bodies and would see for themselves if their body is in a high enough space to enter the temple / the priestess. The semen was also consumed for its healing properties. Vitamins and nutrients that the men needed. Today this sounds unspeakable for a man to consume his own semen. But why is it, that it is perfectly acceptable for a woman to do so. Many today, thanks to the damaging porn industry, think that a woman should always perform oral sex and swallow her partner's semen. Many practice this even with casual sexual partners. Now that you know much more about sexual flow and energies, can you see how ridiculous that sounds? Even if a woman does chose to have a 'one night stand', (which hopefully you are now more wise about, after reading book 1), why must she drink the semen, the DNA of this man, his sexual energy and life force which will most likely cause damage and chaos in her spirit and womb, if he is not the divine masculine she needs?!

Today men cringe from the thought of drinking their own semen yet expect women to do so. Why?

When in a divine union, it is a blessing to use not only the feminine sexual fluids but the male partner's fluids as well. That is of course if both partners have been through the self – initiation period and their bodies, their vessel, and channel of light are pure, clean, and ready to be used in sexual magic. If you still consume alcohol and especially animal products, please do not practice sex magic! Your bodies are full of low vibration energy of death, pain, fear and trauma and this will of course change and destroy your DNA and sexual fluids. It will create chaos if you wish to use these fluids to manifest anything. You will only attract and create the same low frequency of trauma, fear, and pain- in your lives.

If you have prepared yourself, on the other hand, the semen can be placed in a cup or, the woman would take it in her mouth with love, through oral sex, worshiping the god in her man and transfer it to the man's mouth through a sacred kiss. They both swallow the seed together, focused intensely on their intention or sigil, while practicing breath of life practice (which you can learn about in *Sex Magic Evolution*) and raising their serpents up their spine, awakening their energy body, and releasing the light liquid from their pineal gland. This is usually done only if the priestess indeed sees the man as a god, and knows his body and heart is pure enough. Needless to say, she as well needs to be a pure vessel to hold your life force. If you are a man who has been living the path of the godman but you have sex with a woman who has not been embodying her divine feminine or has a pure vessel, she will destroy your semen- physically and energetically. So again everyone- CHOOSE YOUR PARTNERS WISELY.

Another way to use the semen in sex magic is for the woman to spit the semen into a chalice/ blessed cup and mix it with her blood, then pour it directly into the earth as a gift to the mother. The couple can then have a sexual union on that same sacred earth, blessing it and receiving the blessings from it at the same time. The only limit is your imagination...

The masculine and feminine are both intertwined within each other's body and spirit. We imprint our DNA and frequency on our partners forever. Our sexual fluids are filled with the essence of our entire being, not just our sexual lust or desire. The woman takes into her the man's essence, and the man gives his life force to the woman. Both now are forever influenced by the partner they chose to unite with.

'One-night stands' do not exist.

When you unite- it is always- forever.

THE OUROBOROS

First, let us explore the magnificent serpent.

The snake is both female and male in its form and energy. The body of the snake is masculine, while the mouth of the snake, especially if you look at a wide-open snake mouth- is feminine. It slithers and flexible as the feminine yet extremely focused and grounded as the masculine.
A snake is known to bring death but also brings life. His venom is poison as well as medicine.

The cobra was, and still is, a sacred animal in the temple. It does not act as the cobras of our world today though. No animal consumes another animal within the dimension of the temple. Sounds crazy, but it's true. Remember, our reality is only one out of infinite realities.
In the last days of the temple, men have started killing and consuming animals and so many of the animal species have vanished for the sake of protecting themselves, as the world quickly lowered in frequency.

Our treatment of animals is highly connected to the human state of consciousness on many levels and I will need a whole book just to explain that. Unfortunately, most humans are not even ready to grasp this truth yet, even though, ironically, it is crucial to our evolution and the reality we create around us.

If you are reading this book, you probably heard often in your life of the term we have been discussing earlier: Kundalini energy.

It is the energy that supports all life in a physical body, and it is depicted by a serpent or two serpents.

The Serpents have been worshiped and feared at the same time, for eons. They have been representing a few things to the subconscious mind. Death, life force and energy, as well as representing a very sexual and sensual energy to the psyche.

Therefore together, these subconscious meanings that we have collectively when it comes to serpents, represent a powerful life force that is created through sexual energy and death. That is why we all, in some level, are fascinated by them and fear them at the same time.

The 2 coiled snakes symbolism have been used for thousands of years with different meanings but holds the same powerful seed of information. They are used primarily for depictions associated with health and medicine, as well as danger and evil.

Their image holds both light and dark within our psyche.

The snake itself has a deep meaning for us as humans, as being a being of power as well as danger. A symbol of sin and sensuality. An animal of deceit, that brings death and destruction, yet represents health, medicine, and vitality. A creature that is extremely intriguing and mysterious.

We can see in our culture many times the pictures of the snake wrapped around a cross, inside a chalice, eating its own tail, and united with another snake in an intertwining embrace. These are all clues to the real true meaning of the serpent, and you will understand them as we move along the teachings of the symbols of the temple.

The snake has an obvious phallic symbolism. But If you look inside the mouth of a snake you will see the magnificent resemblance to the female genitalia.

Therefore, the snake represents both masculine and feminine in one body. The complete union. A whole. A feminine on the inside and the masculine on the outside.

Therefore, the Ouroboros has been a pure symbolism for sexual energy since the beginning of time. They are quite literally in their physical form- a mirror for human sexuality. The snake eating itself is the image of a whole sexual union between masculine and feminine.

Everything in nature breathes, just like humans. There is an expansion and a retraction. Everything in nature has sex. All the time.

The masculine and feminine are too polarized forces. Like electricity, the masculine represents the positive and the feminine is the negative.

Like the symbol of the power outlet, the masculine enters the feminine to create power. To create electricity.

This is what the Ouroboros represents. It is life and death. Dark and light. Positive and negative poles.

The female energy is magnetic. (mag-netic. mag-ic. mag-dalene). She is the dark. She is the underworld. The under-waters of the feminine. The cave, cavern, abyss. The abyss is also the subconscious. The female. The power that creates reality.

Snakes that are depicted head to toe in a coiled manner, represent the DNA, which has a similar shape. This also is symbolic to the flow of sexual energy that moves in a circle between a couple's bodies energy centers.

Snakes entangle themselves when they mate for the sake of reproduction. The symbol of the 2 snakes intertwined is one of creation and birth. It is great to use this image when a woman tries to get pregnant and hears the call of her child. The snakes are powerful protection as well as a force for birth and reproduction.

The number 8 is connected to the Ouroboros itself, a secret number in sex magic. we will explore numbers later in this book as well. The number four is the number of the mother herself, a complete number which unites all four aspects of polarities: The divine feminine, the shadow feminine, the divine masculine and the shadow masculine. So, the number 8 double the force of this union bringing it to an infinite stream of energy. An eternal orgasm.

This is where the infinity symbol was originated from in the temple and is used in many places, especially the ceiling and dark corners of the temple.

The serpent also represents the human spinal column and the movement up the spinal column of the Kundalini energy. It represents the ascension of humankind. And the most powerful direct way to ascend as human beings is through our sexual energy and the way we use it.

The Kundalini energy arises from our sexual organs all the way up to our pineal gland in the center of our skull. The Awakening and activating of our pineal gland are essential for our Ascension. The way we are using our sexual energy today, combined with fluoride in the water and toxic foods destroyed and toxified the pineal gland completely, thus destroying the ability for the Kundalini energy to rise up and hindering our ascension process.

SNAKES RISING

We have all seen the images showing the two snakes intertwine around one another climbing up the spine. This is a very similar image to the double helix DNA.

The image of the two snakes Rising is of vital importance in the sex magic Temple and is used from the first level of initiation.

It is basic and crucial to master the energetic movement in the body that are represented by the snakes.

For many people, this mastering takes a long time and plenty of work and focus. The sisters of the temple have warned me that at this day and age this sexual flow mastering might even take longer because most humans have such imbalances of energy and blocks of energy in their body that completely disconnect them from the ability to allow these energies to work and flow properly. Also, there are many people who try working with these energies but do so without the proper purification, preparation, and respect. With no sufficient 'shadow work', and thus, are creating even more chaos in their life and the lives of those they touch.

That is why a healthy clean diet is a crucial basic step for Sex Magic practices for it allows the more natural flow of kundalini energy in the body. Eating low vibration foods will cause heavy blocks and will not allow the release of them in the cells.

Also, practicing this with the ego of one self, even is it may feel good in the moment, will damage the spirit-body connection in the long run.

The coiled snakes as well as the symbol of the ouroboros, hold within them the power of eternity for they are snakes who are eating their own tails. The beginning and the end, life, and death.

The snake is a symbol of the spinal column. The sexual force, kundalini- which rises up the spinal column until it reaches the pineal gland - which is symbolized by the golden egg. Another known symbol in our society, yet very few know its true meaning.

So, the snake rises up towards the egg. This is symbolic of the process in which a spiritual awakening is achieved. Especially through sex.

The pineal gland is represented by a golden egg, which we can see in many depictions and art images with a serpent around it.

A serpent spiraling an egg, which symbolizes the Kundalini that rises and protects the pineal gland, wanting to unite with it.

The Kundalini energy rises up the spine starting in the sexual center, it reaches the pineal gland, where the egg lies, and the head of the serpent symbolically 'eats' the egg. Uniting both masculine (the rising energy of Kundalini represented by the body of the snake) and feminine (represented by the egg which is the pineal gland itself).

The egg represents of course the female reproductive system, not just the pineal gland, so it is the full embodiment of the feminine energy, and once united with the kundalini energy which is the masculine- a human being is completely ascended and so-called 'enlightened'. The human being is free, living his full potential once this union has taken place.

Many of us know the bible story about Jacob who ascends in his dream up the ladder to heaven. This is the same story! The ascension of life force energy to heaven, the flow of energy rising up to the 3rd eye. To heaven (human spiritual ascension). Another famous kid's story holds the same symbolism. Jake and the beanstalk. Jake, who climbs up the long way up towards the sky where he finds a GOLDEN EGG. He then brings this egg (his gift of awakening) back into the earth- into the material world.

THE EGG AND THE SERPENT

The egg of life is the egg where all life comes from. The snake is a symbol of life- of feminine and masculine in full unity, and the egg- the life, the union between them. A space where all potential and life comes from.

This symbol is also connected to human DNA. No wonder, now that we understand what it really is.

You can find this symbol of the snake and the egg in all religious stories or depictions in some way or another because again: using basic, eternal symbols is a powerful thing. Dark magicians on this planet knew this always, even today, but they have been keeping this knowledge only to be used by a small group of people.

The sisters speak:

"In the days of the temple using symbols was common daily knowledge, but now we hope to inspire and awaken it once more so that divine humans can use symbols again in order to heal this planet from the evil that has taken control over their minds.

"The egg is a symbol used in your reality everywhere. It is related to the flower of life, as you call it, and science has begun to explain the natural patterns that exist in everything in nature. mathematics and physics can also show you this, (the golden ratio) but this is not something we neither care about nor wish to go over in this book. Here we wish to inspire you with the temple's power and explain to you in a more magical, energetic, feminine, left-brain way what the symbols are. We wish for you to feel and KNOW, more than we wish for you to understand.

These are 'clues' if you will, that the mother herself left humans to discover, so they can understand that they are connected to all life and that all life is connected to them. That all life comes from the egg, from the womb of the mother, and all life goes back to her."

Our human bodies have been imbalanced for a long time. Everyone has been feeling the imbalance of the feminine and masculine and that has been affecting us on a deep cellular level and spiritual level.

As the process of balancing and union is taking place at this point in time, many may feel intense emotions, fatigue, hallucinations, headaches, a desire to be alone with no people around, to isolate oneself. Many may feel the need to escape this dimension with psychedelic drugs or alcohol. There may be a weakness in the body or even confusion about your own sexuality and even gender.

You must allow the body time to heal and balance. But you must also help your body through cleansing and purification (like juicing and enema), eating a full diet of living, light foods (raw vegan diet is best. But the vegan diet is crucial). You must surround yourself with the right people, choose places and circumstance that are aligned with your well-being, spend enough time in meditation and nature, drink clean water (preferably blessed water as well), and spend enough time in the Sun (with no chemicals or blockers such as sunscreen).

ACTIVATING THE 'GOLDEN EGG'

The activation of the golden egg is in fact the activation of the pineal gland. We have learned in LEVE 1 that the activation happens once the two 'serpents' rise the spine and reach the 3rd eye. But it is best to activate it even before the sexual union even begins.

It is best to keep activating the 3rd eye all day long.

Yes. This is a never-ending connection and intention we must have as awakened humans. There is no other sexual partner or even a spirit lover that can do this for us. We are in full responsibility for our own life force. We are the ones that can KNOW ourselves, and that can SEE through our 3rd eye, our highest soul, and we are the ones who must keep it in the purest, powerful state.

This is why we must keep our vessels, thoughts, heart, and mind pure and clean at all times. The activation of our kundalini is not a one-time thing during some great sex act or ritual. It is a continuous ritual, created by us, for us, and the cosmos, in every moment we breathe. In our awake as well as our sleep state.

3 glands pass through the middle of our bodies in perfect symmetry.

The pineal gland. The thyroid gland (throat chakra) and the penis/portal (pussy).

You can see that our sexual energy, along with our voices and our spirit, subconscious mind, all are in perfect alignment in the line of the body. And for a reason. All are vital for a sacred union. All are needed for a spiritual awakening. And all are constantly creating our reality- magic.

Snakes rely on their nasal sensory organ to survive.

Their smell receptors which are located at the base of the nasal septum and the roof of the mouth are used to detect pheromones and help them connect and transfer information between others. Just like us they use their tongue to explore and feel....kissing is a reptilian act of exchange of fluids, information, and energy.

OUROBOROS

The Uvula, which is located in our throat, is the gate to the mouth. It is a second clitoris. The woman's voice is highly powerful and was one of the things the men saw as dangerous when they began to silence the temple priestesses.

The snake inserting its phallic tail into its own feminine mouth-creates life.
When we kiss- we have liquids in both sets of lips, the fluid aids the movement of energy.
The kiss is the complete circle of energy during sex. It is our second sexual organ.
Both sets of lips represent the ouroboros- the complete cycle of life energy. Of creation.
The sexual organs as well as the mouth are both portals of creation. On one end- The woman's portal where life comes out of, and the penis, which holds the seed of life and creation. On the other end- the human voice. Words, spells- which create the reality we live in. our voice creates sonic energy. Patterns in our reality which structure our material reality.

In the temple, some priestesses could see the actual energy that the voice created. That is why they practiced silence whenever they could, as well as voice activation, and extreme intentional use of their words. Their spells were powerful and enchanting. They could awaken a soul with only their voice. They knew they had the power to destroy as well, so they kept their mind and emotional body always at the highest state and took responsibility for that power.

That is what they taught their initiates and how they lived their lives.

"The human voice is a gift which must be used with responsibility and love. Wisdom spoken must be earned first. Must be mastered. Must be embodied. Otherwise, words are empty, and they can cause destruction. "
                                                    - the priestesses of the temple.

The ouroboros represents rebirth and renewal.
The symbol of the snake eating itself is highly encoded with sexual power. It is, in fact, the essence of sex itself. Because all sexual union occurs first and foremost within us.

It is a symbol for the second level of Sex Magic and the temple, whereas the initiate learns to unite sexually with themselves, and by doing so uniting sexually with the entire universe.
This simple symbol represents a creature who is both feminine and masculine and is performing a divine union on its own.

The Ouroboros represents Infinity as well, and together with the energy of sex, it holds the power for the infinite orgasm which is a part of the teachings of the Sex Magic School on the higher levels. This creature represents the state of mind and consciousness of which the initiate strives to live in constantly.

Our lives as magical humans have been dormant for a long time, but with the age of information the truth is coming out and the true meaning of magic and symbols are rising up within our consciousness. Just like the snake, we are beginning to unite both our light and shadow and raise our life force and true powers into the physical world.

The power of Kundalini is rising again after eons of being asleep and unaware within our DNA. It is not a surprise to the conscious human now that this is also the time when the dark forces are using their finest weapons against us, trying to keep this awakening to occur. Because once a human has experienced his/her awakening, they will never be asleep again, and- they can never be controlled again.

The age of information is bringing us again the apple of knowledge that was once given to us by Lilith herself.
Let us use this knowledge with wisdom and love. Ground ourselves in this physical world with true power and unite Heaven and Earth within us.
Let us create a sacred union that will, in turn, create a new world, a new dimension that fits for kings and queens.
For gods and goddesses.
In the sex magic school, we learn how to rise our Kundalini energy from the lower chakra, from our sexual organs, in the best way, up until the third eye and higher chakras.
We learn to connect our physical body with our spirit and soul uniting the three in a new and whole dimension where our being is complete.

USING THE SYMBOL IN SEX MAGIC?

The Ouroboros is best to be used solitary practices of Sex Magic. It gives the user and initiate the fool wholeness and Power his or her own divine feminine and masculine.
Using this symbol well strengthens both your feminine and masculine and Aid in the transmission of the sexual energies in your body to be moved in the right direction without the need for another person to be your partner.

The Ouroboros is also very helpful to unite a Divine couple when they wish to regenerate their bond and Union. It is a sort of renewal of vows if you wish. Used to keep and strengthen a certain specific energy that the couple already has together.

You can use the symbol of the Ouroboros in the shape of a circle or a shape of the number 8 (or the infinity symbol). Depends on your specific desire to manifest or your energetic needs in that specific sexual ritual you are creating.

A Circle will be used more to create something new and send it to the ether, while the infinity symbol will be used to strengthen and re-generate any existing energies or vibrations.

Like any other symbol, you may draw it right on your altar or on the body or the forehead of your lover.

When using this symbol alone you may simply imagine it or even draw it on your body. For example, you can draw it on your third eye or on your thigh, just above your knee, so if you are laying down or sitting on your knees you can see it clearly in front of you. You can draw it on each other to have a clear view during orgasm.

You may also draw it on a piece of paper and place it underneath your pillow. Sleep with it under your pillow until the next morning where you can either burn it or bury it. Depends on what feels right to you.

Another method is to work with water, and you can draw the symbol on your bottle of water or tape a piece of paper with the symbol drawn on it, on your bottle of water. You can place it underneath a bottle of water. Preferably a glass bottle and place it for 24 hours under a full moon and under the sun and then leave it on your altar for as long as you like. This fills the water with not only the power of the symbol itself but the powers of the Sun and the Moon- the masculine and feminine- you are filing and restructuring the molecules of the water together with the symbol, creating extremely powerful, healing, and magical waters.

You may also use the symbol of the two serpents feeding off each other's tails, in a circle, or in an infinity shape. It is best used in a divine union, for the intention of a physical birth. If you are ready and have heard the call from a new soul that wants to be birthed through you.

These two serpents will help bring the new baby in a safe way from the other dimensions into your body. make sure you are conceiving this child within a circle and inside a pyramid. yes- a child in the temple was conceived in a very intentional, intricate way. you want to create a space that holds completion, full divine union, and eternity.

For more knowledge on how to bring a magical child into this dimension through sex magic, can be found in the sex magic school.

LILITH

You may wonder why Lilith is mentioned in this book. 'Lilith is a woman, not a symbol' you may think, but you would be wrong.

LILITH is one of the most ancient symbols there is. If not the most ancient symbol. Since she is the prime earth mother of us all. Holding the feminine light codes through all time and generations.
Her symbol has been used primarily by the dark masculine world- which we can call the dark lords- she has been used as a demonic symbol to take away our powers.
You see, any symbol, when used in an inverted way, will still emit the powers it has but- you guessed it- in an inverted way. So, they took her image and distorted it until it was completely the opposite of who she truly was. But now, she is back. She actually never left but we couldn't connect to her since we have been so much in the shadows.

Lilith is more than any symbol there is. She holds us all in her blood. She holds our true power. She is the first woman, encoded with the feminine' s true power. She is you. She is me. She awakens us all now not only to unite all fragmented parts in us, but she reminds us of the divine mother in us all.

THE STORY OF LILITH AND EVE

We know now that the serpent has been demonized, but there is another woman who is related to the serpent in the stories of religion. A woman, whom according to the dark lords, is even more evil and more dangerous than the serpent itself. Her name was LILITH.

Any bible or religious book is filled with inconsistencies and contradictions. Books of lies, compiled from small truths, put together in a web of manipulation and spells. Stories that are written by men, who were all guided by the dark masculine force. The bible is a book that has changed many times over the years to serve the agenda of the lying men or entities at that specific point in time.

The first story of the bible, the basis of all other lies, is the story of Adam and Eve. We all know it. Even those who never grew up around religion know who Adam and Eve were.

This story teaches us that a woman is to blame for the fall of man and is therefore cursed with the pain of childbirth. It was *she* who was weak, tempted by an evil snake instead of listening and following her man, which, by the way, she was created from, and for the purpose of his amusement, so he wouldn't be alone and bored in the Garden of Eden.

This story has another version though. With a character who is often forgotten and not mentioned.

Lilith.

In the Jewish Midrash (which is another interpretive book that tries to explain all the contradictions in the bible), and in the

Kabbalah, Eve wasn't Adam's first wife. Lilith was. She was banished and replaced by Eve, the more subservient, weak, submissive one. Lilith was wild and opinionated. She did not follow or bow down to Adam, for he was birthed from her womb, who is connected to the eternal womb of the mother. She always knew who she was. Her worth and endless love, therefore she was not only banished but forgotten. And later when she wasn't able to be forgotten, she was demonized, and her image distorted. Fits perfectly with the agenda of the dark masculine world that they wanted to create, don't you think?

Some versions of the story say Lilith herself was the snake, that she was evil, and tried to seduce Eve into tasting the fruit of knowledge.

One day, I asked the Mother to show Lilith to me. From what I have seen, Lilith did, in fact, want Eve to taste that fruit, but there was nothing evil about it.

What Lilith tried to give Eve was knowledge, wisdom, freedom to live in her own natural power and pleasure. Her intention was of sisterhood. Not vengeance for the fact she was banished. In fact, she was never banished. She ran away. She fled Adam and his domination of her. She saw the world he was about to create and wished to create herself in another dimension where she can live eternally and guide all women that will follow. Eve did not wish to join her, so Eve was the one who has been holding the light codes to women of our reality all this time. She remained within this timeline!

Lilith is entering this dimension again now through us, sisters. But we need to open the gates for her to enter. We must connect with her once more.

Sisters, if you have been through the full initiation with book 1- then I have no doubt you are already feeling and embodying her energy right now.

Lilith wants to remind us we are the Creators. That we, women, are the guides to sexual union. Our domain is sexuality. We hold the womb- the entire universe, quite literally- inside of us.
Lilith wanted to awaken Eve to the way Adam saw her and used her so that Eve could find her own freedom. I would have done the same for any sister of mine. Wouldn't you?

I personally don't believe in the bible or any religion. I see them for what they are- weapons of the dark masculine- and they have been very successful ones, but they are falling apart. The time of the Mother is the time of truth. It surfaces and cannot be stopped.

That said, I see Lilith and Eve as archetypes. Symbols that our collective consciousness has created for ages. They are both one. They represent two (but not the only), aspects of the feminine.

Lilith had been hidden from us until the last few years. More and more mention her name because her spirit is returning to life in all women.
Adam is a symbol of the patriarchy and Lilith refused to be dominated by its power, escaped, and was called the mother of all demons. A child killer.
Religion has lied and twisted the image of her because religion is the main weapon that the dark masculine has, along with many other weapons- such as- food, sex, destruction of imagination, of childhood and the family unit, and so much more...

LILITH IF OUR FIRE. She is the wild, untamed, freedom seeker in all of us. She is colorful, unstoppable, and brings out our desire, passion, and even lust. She is bursting in our wombs now. She is one of my sisters in the temple of Isis, guiding me with Isis herself. I love feeling her spirit. It is very similar to mine, but I also have learned from her that I am not complete without Eve.

Eve allowed Adam to rule her, but she is awakening as well now. In her darkness, she was a man's object, but her spirit is one of serenity, allowing, motherhood, gentleness, caring. With a divine masculine by her side, Eve can be the full embodiment of the divine feminine aspect that holds surrendering, releasing, receiving, nurturing. (The problem was that Adam was the embodiment of the childish dark masculine and he was not a divine masculine archetype.)

Eve and Lilith carry all the love that the Mother has within their own divine powers. Lilith and Eve are just two, though the main, aspects of the feminine energy. There are many more aspects to the Mother and to a woman (which you can later explore in level 3 book- *The Sex Priestess Manual*). It is up to us now, to explore every part in us, to embrace them, and create the perfect symbiosis of aspects within us. Create the woman that you really are. And we do this with the most important sister- the one who holds the primordial force of the feminine- LILITH.

Lilith is connected to the menstrual blood which holds immense magic and as such she holds the key to life itself. She holds the knowledge of Divine Magic. She absolutely has the knowledge of the dark powers as well. That is exactly what makes her complete whole and powerful. But because of her wisdom, she knows exactly how to use the knowledge that she has for divine intentions of creation, for she is a servant of the Divine Mother. She is my highest sister of the Temple, and she is my direct connection to the temple itself. She can be your connection as well- to the highest wisdom of the temple- when you connect to her once more.

In the Jewish tradition, she was believed to be the mother of all demons and evil spirits. These are called - sitra ahra (literally translated to: 'the other side')

She has been called a whore, especially by the church. A particularly amusing fact because the church itself is the 'whore of Babylon' once you learn the true meaning behind the symbols of the church itself).

She was called a succubus (female vampire). She was known to kill men and devour them after she made love to them. And the most horrific lie about her was that she killed and ate children.

She's the one who holds the seed of all knowledge and truth (the seed of the Apple), yet she was depicted as the seed of all evil. The root of the dark side of mankind. A danger to us all. We have seen it for ages, how the dark masculine world makes women believe that knowledge is evil and that they should remain meek and focus on childbearing and serving their husbands. The truth is ugly, but this story of Adam and Eve is still playing in this world (and in our psych) in many places, in many ways. We all know this; some people simply choose to ignore this for the sake of a false feeling of safety or security. But knowledge, combined with true wisdom and love, is the safest thing for us. We must awaken once more to the true power of our divine feminine, for it must awake as well, in return, the divine masculine.

Knowledge is information. Information is light. Light is what will banish the darkness.

We will no longer blindly believe the story the dark masculine world has created for us to believe.

LILITH holds the wisdom of the womb and the power of the Sacred Blood, which flows naturally from the eternal womb. It is not blood that is taken by force, sacrifice or by pain, but the blood that is given freely by the body in a natural cycle. Therefore, we can connect to Lilith better in times of bleeding, and with the moon cycles. She holds the secrets of the true power of the blood of life that flows in and through all women.

LILITH wishes to connect all of us, all sisters, and bring us back to the temple once again.

LILITH is the one who gave Eve an apple and the tree of life is a tree of knowledge. Of light, not of darkness. The world of the dark masculine has made us believe, through the symbolism of the two trees (the tree of life and the tree of knowledge), that this second tree was bad. But it could not be farther from the truth.

The dark masculine world has been hiding from us, not only divine knowledge but the true power we all hold within us. Raging, loving, ever-changing. Flowing, ecstatic, passionate. A force more powerful than any words of ill intent, of any beliefs or programming. A force more ancient than time itself.

LILITH is the true symbol of the true power of the divine feminine. That is why no matter how much the darkness has tried to destroy her, she will never vanish for she is in us all.

We hold her inside our wombs, dear sisters, and if we listen, we can hear her speak to us.

Connecting with her will connect a switch and wisdom, ancient as time itself. She awakens powers within us that have been lying dormant for too long. She connects us to each other. She connects us to the temple, and the Mother herself.

LILITH is the primal feminine force. She holds the mysteries of the feminine, the pain, and the longing. She reminds us of the secrets of the divine union that we all hold.

LILITH is a connection to the astral plane as well. To the subconscious deepest shadows most humans will never find the courage to face. She opens the portals to mystical experiences and awakens the life force within us. In men and women alike.

LILITH will show you how to live as the goddess that you are, how to make love, and use your sexual powers as they should be used. And how, with your divinity- to awaken the divine masculine as well.

She holds both shadow AND light. And she teaches us to accept and own all of it. In a way, she is the feminine symbol that is the closest to the divine mother herself. and just like the feminine energy itself- have been depicted as evil in the dark masculine world.

NOTE: Many dark practitioners today still use her symbol and energy for baneful magic. LILITH has told me how she dislikes this fact. That she is never aiding one who wishes to use her powers for evil or baneful intentions. She will never cause them any harm, but she is NEVER the one who is evoked by such people. If one evokes her while having negative or low-frequency intentions- anything less than love, really- they are actually evoking demons. Not her spirit.

LILITH holds love and anger, rage and passion. Life and death. She is fire, life, rebellion. She a symbol of women's sexual freedom. She is the free matriarchal energy that refuses to be dominated or controlled and she is awakening in all women.

Eons of hatred have not yet destroyed her connection to us. We all still feel her, in one form or another, and in this time, she wishes to connect with us, and through us, once again. To guide us into our own powers and unity.

LILITH is an inspiration to us all and a reminder to never stop seeking our true power no matter what it costs us. Even if we are cast, abandoned, dominated, or demonized. She wishes to bring back justice and liberation from the shadow patriarchy and to bring us back into alignment with our own soul evolution.

LILITH reminds us of the deep wound the feminine is holding since the beginning of time- the wound of rejection, separation, and abandonment from the masculine.
But with this neglect from the masculine, we find our own power and sovereign place in this world. She reminds us to always be authentic with ourselves, to never feel ashamed about who we are and about our true power. Lilith is the first woman, and she is a part of all of us which should tell us how worthy we are and how valuable we are no matter what this reality might tell us.

LILITH is the cord that binds us all in an eternal circle of wombs. She has been demonized mostly from us, sisters. To bring fear within our soul. To pull us apart from her, but that fear is pulling us apart from each other and from our true feminine power. It is time to rise and call upon her. To bring her back to life in this dimension, through our bodies, through our wombs. It is time to connect to true divine power and Lilith is our primary connection to it.

CALLING UPON LILITH IN OUR SEX MAGIC PRACTICE

LILITH holds the power of the snake- which represents the kundalini energy, uniting, and rising within each partner and between them as they unite. Evoking her or imagining her during a sexual union will strengthen both partners and the union itself.

Work with the energy and guidance of Lilith, great sisters. In your own individual work and practice, as well as in your sexual union with your partner. Call her, communicate with her, speak to her. She will answer. If you are ready to listen and if you can hold her frequency.

Make sure you are prepared. Pure vessel, heart, and mind. With love and intentions of awakening and truth. If you are not ready to hear the truth, if your vessel is not clear enough, Lilith will not hand you the 'apple'.

She is inside you and me and she is longing for us all, sisters, to connect with her once more. You do not need me or anyone to communicate with her. Trust your womb and your heart and speak to our first sister/earth mother.

She loves us all. She awaits you.

LILITH appreciates sisterhood and will communicate well when you have the circle of your sisters in your life. Cultivate and feed healthy sisterhood around you. Evoke Lilith together or apart, she will feel your power and love and desire to connect through the womb to her and the mother and she will speak to you in ways you never dreamed of.

For those of you who wish to be initiated as a sex priestess in the temple, you will also learn to evoke Lilith and permit her to unite with your partner as well.

But for now, just speak to her. You know how. You have always known. Hold both hands on your womb and speak to her. FEEL her. Know her.

When in a sexual union with your partner, ask her if she will be willing to bless your union. If she says no- well, that should tell you a lot about the union you are in.

Make sure to invoke her within the circle, as taught in book 1- and practice safe magic with protection, banishing, and most of all- pure heart and intentions.

THE ANKH

The Ankh is considered to be the Egyptian symbol of life and immortality, but there is so much more to this magical sigil. It was mainly used in the temple as the symbol of the union between man and woman. It is called as well- the key of the Nile because it represents the union of Osiris and Isis. ISIS was believed to flood the river of Nile thus bringing fertility to Egypt, but in truth, the 'river' represents something else entirely.

Isis was showing me the true 'River'. The divine liquid that flows like a river from the womb itself. Today, we have a different word for it- squirting.

This act of pure release of liquids from the female's body holds a sacred and powerful meaning in the temple. The more the feminine is rising now, the more human beings learn once more of this act, though they still are not using it correctly.

In the temple, we shall call this act- the Isis River.

The ankh has had a correlation with water and their life-giving powers, yet it has not been known to most of the true meaning and what kind of water it symbolizes.

This flowing of liquid releases tremendous energy that is stuck in a female's body, helping her to 'lighten up her load' so to speak, to purify the cells of her body from unwanted energy or pain or trauma.

Another tip for cleansing a woman from trauma, especially sexual trauma is Anal sex.

Yes. You read it correctly.

But there is another big BUT coming...

Anal sex can cleanse a woman from sexual trauma ONLY when done correctly.

The area of the anus holds and stores many emotions and fears, for men as well as women. It is highly sensitive and must be approached with patience and tenderness. Begin to see this area of the body like a secret room that stores deep secrets, wounds, and pain. It can be highly damaging if penetrated by the wrong partner or one that does not feel into your pain and truly wants the best for you. Anal sex must be done with a partner who you feel truly sees you and that you would entrust with your heart. Because you are allowing them to enter a place where you keep hidden emotions, memories, and fears that even you may not know of.

Now let's get back to the Ankh.

The ankh is called 'the key to the underworld' because of this reason as well.

It is the underworld of flowing water that the feminine experiences in the act of the Isis River (squirting) that aids her in transforming her body into a pure vessel of light.

The men in the temple has been using the Isis River and performing it on the sisters of the temple as often as possible. Even daily. Mostly as a service to these women who gave their lives to serve the temple and all who come there to seek healing, awakening, and divine connection. The Sisters of the temple are holding tremendous amounts of energy in their body. Many sisters hold trauma and pain for other sisters as well, as well as for men, therefore this act is vital and crucial for the release and healing of the priestess's body. A priestess practices constant cleansing and purification. She must. She knows she is a never-ending universe of transmuting energies and life. She must always remain the empty, pure vessel where life can begin and end in...

The Isis River is performed better with the symbol of the ankh itself. The process includes holding the ankh or to draw it on her stomach or on the ground underneath her. There are also specific breathing techniques that are involving the shape of the ankh and the flow of breath imitates the shape.

The Ankh is believed to be a symbol for immortality because the Isis River practice allows the regeneration of the cells in the female body to happen more rapidly and powerfully.
This is a secret no one knows about today.
It is not only the Egyptians who use this symbol but many other sex temples around the world, especially in Europe.

The ankh is a sort of a magic wand as well. It reverberates the energies from the orgasm and helps to either hold them in the circle itself or to collect the energy from the orgasm into the circle and then, with the priestess power and spells, to be released into the cosmos where it is used for whatever intention it is needed for.

The Ankh represents the union of divine masculine and feminine. Of the penis and vulva. But more so the power and energy of the orgasm, and can be used as a tool to manipulate and control those energies and power.

The horizontal line represents the division between Heaven and Earth while the vertical represents heaven itself on the top (the divine feminine energy, which seeks to ground) and the Earth on the bottom (the Divine masculine energy which seeks to connect to source- through its connection to the feminine).

The ankh is connected as well to the third eye. When placed between the eyes of the Priestess it can help 'see' beyond this physical world and it is used as a portal for divine sight and guidance for the temple priestesses and men who serve and learn and heal within it.

The priestesses of the temple used this symbol to 'test' a true power of a male initiate and their true intentions.

ISIS has shown me how in the caves of the Temple the initiate would have to sit down in front of a priestess for long periods while she will observe him and look deep into his soul for his true intention. She would draw this symbol on her third eye, or she will draw the symbol on the initiate heart to see clearly into his heart.

This would also be used to choose a new Priestess in the same way. Not every woman would be chosen to be initiated into the temple, therefore, this initial ' test' was performed on females as well.

The Ankh has been used by humans for many wrong reasons.

Many have believed it would give them immortality or power to control others. This of course didn't work because this symbol has a specific energy field and can only move and manipulate energy in specific ways. Since it was created and seeded in the temple of ISIS, no one could have used this tool for any other way. Many still try but this symbol is extremely powerful and protected by its creators. The Sisters of the Temple.

The only way that the ankh can be used for eternal life, is at the moment of orgasm. That is the second when life and death happen at the same time. When energy is created and dying at the same time. The misunderstanding of this symbol is vast, and the sisters of the temple wish to explain and clarify this symbol once and for all.

This symbol absolutely holds the power of life for it holds the power of the orgasm- which holds the power of life and creation itself.

When drawn by a priestess or a man who has been initiated into the temple, it can create a form of protection as well but that is not the main intent for this symbol.

The symbol was tattooed on men who have been initiated into the temple and that was a sign for them that they have reached a level of divinity and divine masculine power within themselves. Some priestesses who chose to mark this symbol on their bodies as well as with the symbol of the coiled snakes.

There have been a few different symbols created that are similar to the ankh, which was given specific meanings by other people throughout history, but this is the meaning and the power of this symbol as it was used in the temple of Isis.

USING THIS SYMBOL IN SEX MAGIC

The deeper teachings of uses of this symbol were taught in the sex Magic temple of Isis and Lilith, to the initiates who have cleansed enough of their physical and energetic body, but here I will give you a few ways that you can begin to use it right now.

* Read the book- *Sex Magic Evolution* to learn the basics of the initiation of sex magic mastery and prepare your vessel for the seeding of this knowledge in your reality.

* Make sure, just as with the use of any symbol of the temple, that when you use this symbol, your body is completely cleansed from low vibrational substances- such as dairy, meat, or any animal products and any ego-mind drugs such as alcohol and cocaine.
Do not use this symbol if your body is not clean from these horrific poisons! This is vital.

* Make sure that you cleanse your body for at least 8 weeks before using this symbol in sex Magic. If you do not follow these instructions, you may cause severe damage to the physical cells of your body or provoke your shadow side in an unhealthy manner that can cause destruction in your life.

* Protection
When you wish to send physical healing to a loved one, you can either place a picture of the person you wish to send healing to on your altar and place this symbol under or next to the picture. You can have a physical ankh or a picture or image of an ankh.
On the time of the orgasm focus on the picture and imagine the energies coming from your own body and orgasm into the bottom of the Ankh, rising and exploding into the top of the Ankh -which is that circle on top- and see that energy explosion entering that person. Therefore it would be wise to use a physical Ankh, big enough so that at least the head or the body of the person in the picture will fit into the circle above the Ankh.

* Calling The Sisterhood

Another way you can use this symbol- (and again make sure your body is clean for at least 8 weeks and ready for transmission of this energy)- is when you wish to call upon the sisters of the temple and work with their energy.

You MUST make sure your intentions are pure, your heart is clear, that you have no expectations other than a pure connection with the divine sisters' energy. You must trust that they will guide you only if you absolutely need the guidance. And once the orgasm has been achieved and you envision it going into the Ankh, you may speak to the sisters, with a spell of gratitude and invitation such as this:

"Dear Sisters of the Temple, I give you my life force,
I ask to unite with my own soul in the temple once more.
I humbly thank you for the guidance and the wisdom."

What you wish to do is show them your true heart, ask for guidance, but also show them that you trust yourself, that you trust the process, that you know yourself. That you are ready for this connection. You show them and the temple you have been preparing your vessel and you have, at least somewhat, mastered the flow of your orgasm and the intention you direct it towards.

SPIRAL AND TRISKELION

The main purpose of a Divine Union and of Sex Magic itself is to create a portal.

It is to bring a possibility into manifestation, unite 2 dimensions into 1.

The spiral is the purest manifestation of an energetic portal, in a physical form and shape. It is the way we can see with our eyes what the portal's movement looks like within another sphere. It is no surprise that the spiral is associate with shamanism and altered states of consciousness.

Spirals are found in nature all over. Spirals are some of the oldest geometric shapes, found carved in caves and tombs, especially in Europe, and can be found carved on rocks around the world.

The temple has some carvings of the Spiral especially in the corners of the cave walls. The Sisters of the temple explained to me that this is because the initiates need to stay in a very focused and grounded State of mind in the temple. That is why there are more markings of a triangle, which helps the subconscious do just that. There are not many spiral markings on the walls especially on the upper Temple, because the spirals draw the subconscious mind as well as the conscious mind into another state and even dimension. In the lower pyramid temple, the one that is inverted underneath the ground, you can find more spirals, especially in the spaces where the sexual rituals are made. There, they are painted, in a larger size, in the middle of the walls, usually inside the diamond (which we will be discussing later).

In this section of the Temple, you will find more symbols of the triple spiral- which humans today call the triskelion.

We've already briefly discussed the meaning of the number 3 in Sex Magic, and we now understand better the nature of the Spiral. So, this should already give you a clue and a deeper understanding to the symbol of the triskelion.

It combines the powers of the divine feminine and masculine and the world they create together, forming a more powerful and direct energy.

How to open a specific portal or draw energy from a specific portal?

The initiates would use their imagination to place their physical bodies in the center of a triskelion. This, combined with the power of the pyramid that they placed their bodies inside of as well, and together with the other teachings and tools that they have earned by initiation and the mastery of their imagination- creates the most unbelievable tremendous power and force. This method is used only by the highest initiates in the temple and will not be discussed in this book.

The triskelion is another symbol which can be inverted, for the directions of the Spiral makes a huge difference on whether the energy is being drawn in or out the bodies of the initiates.

"Many believe this to be a symbol of the Celtic tradition, but in fact, this

symbol reaches far back into your time-space reality. It reaches back into the timeline of the temple itself. " – These are the words of the sisters of the Temple. I never gave this symbol too much thought, but when they spoke these words to me, I could feel their energy and the truth behind them, and I could feel the frequency of this symbol.

" *The Celtics have used this symbol in a very honorable way yet not in the most effective way. This is very similar to the use of many symbols by humans since the beginning of the dark masculine time. Before that, when the goddess was revered and honored, human beings still held knowledge of how to use these symbols in the right way.*"

The sisters of the temple continue to give me more information about the symbol. It appears they wish for me to know a lot more about this symbol, even more than the other ones. I feel their energy almost pressing.

"*The Catholic church has tried to use this symbol but because the symbol is too powerful for the low vibration religion has created on this planet, it did not take so much hold in the art of the Catholic Church, and this symbol does not hold power when drawn by a human being with the intention for malefic use of it. Although the church cannot use this symbol in the way that they wished to, others in society have been able to pull and use the power from this symbol in malefic ways. They have done so by dark magic such as sacrificial blood use, and the use of modern-day technology combined with spells, which create portals that control the subconscious of human beings- what some would call- brainwashing and programming. These individuals and groups have used inversion with this symbol and mostly use it in order to pull away life force from the subconscious mind of humans.*"

As I listen to my sisters speak through me I do not feel fear. I feel tremendous power entering me as I am receiving this knowledge and information, especially because I know I am about to share it with people and this knowledge is vital in our Awakening process.

I asked my sisters about the use of this symbol right now and how we can use it correctly. This is what they say:

"First, you must connect to the symbol by yourself. You must envision which direction the spiral turns according to your imagination in order to draw energy in. You must remember this direction and use it later on again and again. Use the palm of your hand to move in a circle and a spiral. First, circle your wrist to the right side. Feel if the energies are moving inward or outward – towards you or away from your body- feel if you are moving energy towards inside your body and into your hand, or are you pulling energy out."

As I do this, I feel energy pulled in my body as I turn my wrist to the right side. This is something I've been doing for years naturally and now the sisters of the temple are actually explaining it in a more precise manner, so I feel very connected with this information, and I feel confidence as I receive this powerful, clear confirmation.

"When you draw or use this symbol make sure that the spiral is moving towards the direction that pulls energy towards your body. The other direction is the inverted one. You can use a spiral moving to the other direction in order to push things away from your life, to pull energy out and clean your body. You can use the power of your orgasm while looking directly into the middle of this symbol. We recommend you use the color gold for this symbol if it is available to you, simply because it awakens the specific codes of the symbol in the best way possible. You may choose any color, of course, the gold was used by the temple for its very high frequency and power."

The sisters of the temple wish to remind to all who are reading this book, to always make sure to use any magic and spell with the right, benevolent intentions and never use it to harm anyone or anything. The only person you will harm is yourself, and you will also create a tremendous amount of energy transformed back to you at some point in time- this is what human beings call- Karma. And it applies especially when intentionally trying to use magic, sexual magic, or sacred symbols. This is why it is so important to take the time for self-initiation and prepare yourself- body, heart, mind, and spirit.

THE DIAMOND
THE SYMBOL OF THE TEMPLE

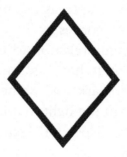

As you can see, this symbol, given to me by the sisters of the temple, is known to us as the diamond.

This symbol is not the one that has been used in the temple, but one that has been created for us, for the ready humans of this space-time to receive the codes in the best way.

I will explain more about the specifics of this symbol and will show you how to use it for your own unique empowerment and re-programming work. This is a vital symbol that will change your life if you use it correctly.

So let us begin with the diamond:

What is a Diamond?

Diamond is rare. The hardest known natural substance, naturally occurring mineral that has the strongest type of chemical bond. Resistant and durable, one that can cut through metals.

Diamond also has special optical properties such as a high index of refraction, high dispersion, and high luster. These properties help make the diamond the world's most popular gemstone and enable it to be used in specialty lenses where durability and performance are required.

Diamonds form below the surface of the earth, about 100 miles below, not on the earth's surface itself. They form at high temperatures and pressures. Most diamonds were brought up to the surface by volcanic eruptions. Many of the real diamonds are delivered to earth in meteorites.

Diamonds have a unique reaction to light, more than any other gemstone, causing them to have optical properties.

The reason for their spark and shine is the ability they must reflect a high amount of the light that hits their surface. They can also be due to high dispersion, separate white light into its component colors. Because they are very hard, they are often used for cutting, drilling, or grinding hard materials.

THE GIFT OF THE DIAMOND

The symbol of the diamond, according to the sisters, represents the earthly commitment one holds to his life purpose.

The very basic art and ability to maintain balance within the individual. The union of body and spirit. Balance and union between the feminine and masculine in one's being, which affect the entire world.

It holds codes of clarity and focus. The ego and spirit combined into one purpose. This is of course very similar to the Merkava, but this symbol is a more grounded one, a more solidified within this physical world than the Merkava, which is a vehicle that takes you to higher realms.

The diamond is also used for more solitary sex magic and can hold the physical and energetic body of the initiate alone, while the Merkava is best used in sex magic, to hold two bodies within it. Again- a reminder, you must not use the Merkava if your bodies are not at the absolute highest frequency possible and if your connection as partners is not solid and strong. You can use the diamond at any time, alone, to raise your frequency and it is not only great protection and container for your vessel but as a space where you can receive the light codes and information YOU are ready for at that specific moment in time.

The diamond gives us the courage to face our shadows. Which are always representative and mirroring in the external world we are observing.
As above- so below. As within- so without.

It reminds us that what is outside of us is always within as well.
It gives us spiritual maturity. Honesty. Mostly within ourselves.
It helps us work with our ego a lot better.

It is the symbol of Ascension and higher wisdom. Together with clarity and focus, the wisdom can be unstoppable.
It is a metaphysical symbol with alchemical properties that hold all the four elements: fire, earth, air, and water.

Because diamonds are made from carbon they are extremely connected to the physical world and to the power we hold as physical humans. It is connected to matter itself.

The way a diamond reflects light is symbolic of the way our

enlightened Spirit can reflect light into our external world around us.

When we are in an elevated state of consciousness, when we are awakened, when our energy is at its highest frequency, the colors of our aura shine bright. Brighter than a diamond even. But the diamond is a reminder for us to keep our frequencies always elevated and pure.

The sisters explain that diamonds are not meant to be taken out of the earth, like many other crystals they are inside the earth for a purpose. They keep energetic balance, send frequency waves into our atmosphere, and protect the earth itself.

They send information to plants and small animals that live on the earth, and when we steal crystals and diamonds from the earth, we do it (and ourselves) great harm.

Today diamonds are being taken out of the earth in horrific ways. Taking advantage and even torturing many human beings, mostly young children, in particular places on the planet.

Just like we (the sisters of the temple and I) have asked you to be aware of the 'food' that you are eating and the damage it causes the beings that it is taken from (animals), we asked human beings to be very conscious of purchasing crystals and diamonds.

A crystal is a GIFT from the Earth, one that is made to find YOU. Not the other way around. You do not need to sell it in stores and pay for it. You must leave it alone in the earth and if one crystal or rock calls you to pick it up, and you ask for permission to take it with you- only then, can you assume possession of it. And even that is usually only for a period of time because most crystals and gemstones find their way back to the earth or wish to go to another human that needs them the most. Have you ever had a special stone and have lost it suddenly?

Probably this happened many times. It is because stones, like any other part of the earth, is never meant to be 'owned' by anyone. It is meant to flow and move to the place or person that needs it the most, and eventually, it is meant to be back in the earth, if it was taken from it.

Use the diamond as a symbol. A shape. A sigil that holds information and power. A power which now you understand. Using a physical diamond will give you nothing, while the use of the diamond as a sacred symbol is endless for your awakening journey.

In the diamond, we have the triangle which represents the 3 pillars of the sex priestess: knowledge, wisdom, and love. And – Joy, being the fourth added corner with another lower triangle (which forms a diamond)- together this creates a full, empowered human being. Connected to their highest spirit, yet firmly grounded in this reality.

THE DIAMOND AND THE TEMPLE

This section will be completely channeled from the divine Sisters of the Temple. I do not know which sister exactly channeled this message through me, they usually come as one force and speak through me when they wish. This is not something I control or want to control. I absolutely love when they speak through me and I have given myself to them and to the temple, to truth and to the divine mother herself.

This is an explanation about the shape of the diamond as it is used as the symbol of the Temple in the way that it has been

shown to me.
The sisters of the Temple begin:

"As you can see from the symbol- which is a sigil that holds the essence of the power of the Temple- the diamond is the main shape that holds the energy within it. The two triangles represent the physical structure of the Temple. The two pyramids standing on top of the other. The Divine masculine on top of the divine feminine. The feminine steady in the ground, in the cave, in the womb of the mother, where all magic happens. Where the subconscious of the initiates is being transformed, tested, where the dark unites with the light that comes from above. And the upper triangle, which draws the light from the universe itself inside the temple. The place of the masculine. This triangle not only draws light in, but also shoots the energy that is formed in the lower triangle, in the womb, outwards into the universe. The powerful energy forming from the initiates and the divine sex magic union is being sent out upwards through the upper pyramid.
The upper pyramid also connects the lower pyramid with the Outside world. It brings us the energy codes and the state of the collective consciousness of humans so we will know what sort of rituals and magic to work next with and how we can assist in the ascension process and healing of the planet, from within the temple.
This is the divine magic of the Temple. This is what the initiate is preparing themselves for. This is the work and the purpose of our being and our union. We give our all to this mission.

"If you wish to be a true initiate of the Temple, you may draw the symbol in a very visible place in your home or your altar. Begin connecting with this symbol. With the two pyramids and the vortex spiral in the middle."

I wanted to share, as an example, the symbol I drew for myself with the guidance of the sisters. I will not show it to you because it is also encoded with other symbols that are personally mine, but I will describe the main parts of it so you can perhaps get some inspiration when you prepare your own symbol. At the last page of this book you will find space to create and draw your own personal sigil.

So, in my symbol, (which is always placed on my altar, and I also take it with me anywhere if I travel the world) the diamond and spiral in the middle are the main symbols. I added the ouroboros, the star (of David), the chalice, and the ankh around it where it felt right, and I also added my own symbols like the initial of my name and my own personal sigil, as well as an arrow with flowers, that represent many things for me personally.

I also tattooed this symbol on my left arm, as well as other symbols, (but by any means am I suggesting you need to do the same. I am simply sharing my own way of using the symbols). The sisters will continue the explanation of how to create your own unique signature sigil. They refer to my own sigil but I feel you can get inspired from their words when you create your own:

"The two snakes above the copper pyramid (I drew my pyramid in this color) represent the perfect union of divine masculine and feminine in the Kundalini energy that rises the initiate spine and spirit. And the horizontal line between the two snakes above the top pyramid forms a sort of an ankh which stimulates the energy from the temple into the ether through the serpent energy.

On the bottom, you can see the Chalice which holds the entire temple itself. The flower on the bottom is a symbol that represents who we, specifically, chose to bring this knowledge through- Luna Ora. She chose a flower to represent her energy, but she can always change this symbol as she changes in her evolution in life.

You may change this symbol on the bottom beneath the Chalice, and add your own unique symbol to it, and by doing so connect with the temple itself and combining your energy with the temple's.

So, draw the symbol just the way it is exactly (the diamond with the spiral inside), *except the symbol underneath the Chalice which you can change as you wish or leave it as it is if you wish to connect with your Earthly teacher- Luna Ora. But we do recommend you create your own symbol on the bottom of the diamond. "*

They have spoken these words when I was thinking of sharing the image of my personal symbol, but because I have decided not to, I just want to clarify that the main symbol to draw is the diamond with the spiral inside. The other symbols can be drawn around it as you wish as well as adding your own personal sigils.

I hope you can see now how drawing this symbol and combining your own signature energy with that of the temple itself creates the ultimate sigil that can guide you and awaken the light codes that are dormant within your own subconscious mind. This is how to use the diamond and other symbols of the temple, all united and combined with your own mark.

Blessings of love and true divine power, from myself and the temple.

THE 'ALL SEEING EYE'

This all society has been built on sacred symbols. Many of the human anatomy and the star movement. we will only focus on the symbols of the temple here, but I felt a mention of this symbol was needed and the sisters confirmed.

It might surprise many of you that the symbol of 'the eye' or the *Eye of Ra* doesn't have a particular meaning as a sex symbol in the temple. It does not hold great significance, nor it has been used in the temple.

The sisters explain to me and had shown me that this symbol has been mostly used in a much later time and was mostly used by those who desired to control others. It is not necessarily a negative symbol, but it was absolutely used for more malevolent purposes, and it was used more by male individuals. Many of those men seek to take hold of the power of the goddess and to redirect the powers and energy on the planet from a feminine to a masculine one.

The 'eye' symbolizes 2 things. The vagina- a woman's sacred portal and the pineal gland. When this symbol was created these men manipulated many ideas and other symbols (such as the all-powerful yoni and pineal gland) into this sigil and combined their dark magic to control the power inside the pineal gland of humans.

Many do not know the true meaning of the *Eye of Ra* and the origins of its use, and this is primarily because it was created by the same forces that are still controlling the energy of mankind today. Therefore, they do not wish for you to know the true meaning of this symbol. History is only his-story. It's someone else's story and it can be changed and manipulated to fit the current agenda or idea.

Ironically this is one of the most known symbols of the Egyptian culture and is still used today by many other cultures as well.

In the Middle East, this symbol has been used for a long time for protection against the 'evil eye'.

This will explain to you perhaps why this symbol is filled with chaos and control and violence.

The use of a symbol creates specific vibration and frequency which creates the reality around it. Not knowing the true meaning of the symbol will not change that. Therefore, wherever this symbol is used most often, you will find more violence and chaos.

It is used all over the world today especially in the western world and is seen very often in modern fashion and culture. Many celebrities are using this symbol to spread their power over the masses as well.

Many who use the symbol are not aware of its powers at all and are simply puppets who are being used for the purpose of manipulation of energy.

You may see this symbol inside the shape of a triangle or a pyramid many times. And now that you know the power and meaning of the triangle you can understand how it is used to empower the symbol of the eye and bring more focus to it, hence, empowering the control and manipulation of the subconscious mind of humans.

This symbol used to represent the eye of the goddess and is still believed to be just that, but unfortunately, it has been used to destroy the feminine energy as well. This is a hidden secret that almost no one knows about. The men who wished for the destruction of the temple, used this symbol, among others, to weaken the power of the temple, by manipulating the minds of the people around the temple's walls, poison their minds about all that was sacred. This is a whole other story... which I may share another time.

The Eye of Ra has been used with much force and violence with the intention of controlling and manipulating Energies. This symbol is not found in the temple of ISIS and LILITH.

This symbol will not be found in any Sex Temple.

Though many Cults have used it to worship the goddess in the older times, it has been hijacked by the dark masculine forces and has been used primarily for control since then.

It was NEVER used for the purposes of Sex Magic at any given time in history.

This symbol has been used in very dark and ritualistic celebrations of dark forces. More importantly, it was created with dark intentions- which is all that matters. The birth of a symbol is what programs it to its core, forever.

It was (and still is) used to worship and evoke malefic entities and show respect to those entities while showing the total control over the human psyche. The Sisters of the Temple wish for me to call these entities what they truly are- demons.

The sisters:

"The truth must be revealed now, and the specific correct words must be used in order to describe and explain the nature of the hidden knowledge of symbols. Many people today have tattooed this symbol on their bodies, unknowingly giving their powers away. When one tattoos their body, it creates a blood sacrifice, which empowers any symbol that you may tattoo on your skin. Therefore, when a person tattoos such a symbol on their skin, they are announcing to these demons that they are an open portal to be used by them. by giving the offering of blood to the symbol, they are completely giving their powers away."

"The eye represents the all-seeing eye of the dark energy, which is able to see all the 'lost children' and in a way, bring them back under the control of the dark masculine. Of the malevolent father. The controlling God-image that has been painted by the dark masculine energy. Ingrained in the deep psyche of mankind. This was meant to control, punish, and manipulate Humanity."

For many, the Eye of Ra has been a representation of the Sun. The sun, which holds the true power of life and destruction within it. Many see it as a symbol of royalty, and therefore they worship and wish to use the symbol often.

I asked the sisters of the temple if there is any way to use this symbol in an inverted way and create positive energy with it. This is what they explained:

"You can absolutely invert any symbol, but at this point in human time-line, this symbol has been used too much by dark forces and it is completely taken by this energy. Therefore, we would not recommend using this symbol at all. There is no need for it right now. It is used too much and the energy of it has been hijacked completely by the rulers of Your World. At this point, we would recommend creating new sigils and symbols in order to bring light and not focus on the old ones who have been destroying it. There is a difference between the Eye of Ra and the Eye of Horus in the meaning that human beings have given it, but to the

conscious mind, the symbol of the eye has been hijacked completely at this point. Therefore, we highly suggest to not give this symbol any more power any longer. "

So, there you have it. This is also the exact reason why I would not even add the image of the symbol into this book.

Now we know, let's move on to the realm of other kinds of sacred symbols- numbers.

SEX MAGIC NUMBERS

Mathematics can reveal endless universal secrets, but this book will stay focused on simple, focused views of symbols and numbers (which are symbols themselves that hold endless information) from the point of view of the temple itself, in such a way to help you understand the flow of sexual union better and use it in your everyday lives. The simpler the better for the subconscious mind to assimilate the information and re-program itself.

As you are about to see, the understanding of the numbers as they were seen at the temple, is very simple. The priestesses explain to me that in our reality now, one can explore the power of these numbers endlessly, with the knowledge of mathematics, sacred geometry, and even physics, but they wish for humans to KNOW these tools, these symbols, in the simplest way possible so that they can begin to implement their use now in their sex magic practice and everyday life, this will work best with the subconscious mind (remember the subconscious mind works best with simplicity). We are at a point where there is no need to dissect the numbers and symbols, more to FEEL them, and allow their information to guide you.

You already have all knowledge within you, now it is time to use it. With ease. With joy.

Numbers are energetic codes that help humanity in creating the physical reality itself. Since numbers are themselves symbols that carry enormous amounts of energy, we will go over the most important numbers when it comes to sex magic now and explore what energy and frequency each number holds in its use in the temple. This will help us understand much of the flow of sex magic and will add much power to your sexual union rituals.

THE POWER OF 3

In sex, you need 3. No, not a third person. A third energy.

Two together create a world, but they need to connect to a higher spirit/source and have an intention to truly unite and have conscious control over their creation. They must know they are a part of the whole. It is them and the entire world - Man, Woman, and Source, the holy trinity.

When two people are only in it for themselves, unaware (like most humans having sex today), they still create a world together- we always create a world when having sex- the question is, again, WHAT ARE YOU CREATING?

When a couple comes together with an intention, knowing that their union has the power to birth a reality- they arrive at the gate of their sexual union mature, powerful, intentional. And that is a game-changer.

In Hebrew and ancient text of magic (the same texts that the wisdom of the Jewish religion and other religions have been taken from), the holy trinity idea came from. This is where the distorted idea of the Father, Son, and the holy spirit came from.
The number 3 is one of the most sacred balanced numbers.
The number 3 holds a high honor in the sex magic temple, the power of the feminine, the masculine, and source, the divine mother herself- in a sacred triangle that protects and holds the world they create together in a divine way.

The number three has another importance when it comes to sex Magic. You have all heard about the 7 chakra system within our body but really within the temple, it is three main chakras that are important and are constantly being used.
The three chakras are the throat chakra, the heart chakra, and the Earth chakra which is known as the root chakra.
These must be always pure and ready for the transmission and movement of sexual fluids in the best way between the partners.
The throat chakra, as well as the earth chakra, are both in fact mirrors of each other in their energy as well as in their power to birth reality. The words we speak create our reality, birth life into matter- as well as the earth chakra where an actual life is formed by the semen and the egg.

In *Sex Magic Evolution* we learn about the importance of words and spells and our human voices, and it is a vital understanding for the sake of any magic and especially Sex Magic. It is vital to master and understand divine men and women.

Our sexual energy, our voices, and our emotions that come deeply from the heart are the three main ingredients that create all life and all matter. These are the ingredients that create us within this construct of reality. How these three power centers work within our body determines everything within our life and especially Who we are and how we navigate this dimension.

Every number is a sigil on its own, a symbol holding a specific energy and information.

The number 3 creates the triangle, which is a symbol of the pyramid as well.

Male, female, source (the world they create together).

It is the number of manifestation and overcoming duality. It is the basic number of sex magic and the most important one. It is a code reminding the initiates of their commitment to their partner, themselves, and the mother. A focus point. A container of the energy they create together.

THE NUMBER 33

This number is always used in the temple. It is marked on the walls of the temple in its original form, as well as the number 8, which is written with the same lines as 33 but with one of the 3's is facing the other way. It also makes the infinity symbol. This number is used mostly for the initiate men in their time of preparation and cleansing when they are only allowed into the main halls of the temple but not to the deeper chambers. Not yet.

Use this number in this time of preparation and of physical and spiritual cleansing. It will aid you and push you and be a reminder of your commitment. The number 33 is a promise, a commitment to your path, to the path you are manifesting into form. It holds both worlds while grounds you- the world you are in now and the world you are birthing. It represents both triangles- the one that faces upwards and the inverted one

124

beneath- and that means that the number 33 also represents the diamond. You can work with this number as you envision your vessel within the diamond, especially in your solitary work.

The sisters explain: "*When used with your partner, both partners should work with this number at the same time because if only one is focused on it, it will create an imbalance in your energies. You can draw it in a place you both can see it clearly or even draw it on each other's body in a visible place.*"

THE NUMBER 0

The number that usually no one takes into consideration. 0.
It is the circle. It is all of life. The womb. All potential. Without it we are slaves to the system, but with it we have the full spectrum.
We must begin counting at 0. This is the divine feminine that has been suppressed. Forgotten. The hollow womb that is filled with all endless potential of life. All begins in the womb. All created within its borders. All begin at 0.
When you work with the magician's circle you are already connecting organically to this number and its powers, so work with the circle as we have discussed earlier, and you will connect and harness the power of 0.

We have already learned about the next important number in the temple- 3. Using the number 3 in our sexual rituals helps in creating this divine union. In a sacred manner. That is why the temple itself is built within a pyramid- which is in fact four triangles connected. Which leads us to number 4.

THE NUMBER 4

The number 4 represents the divine mother herself. It is the number of the mother.

The four triangles of the pyramid hold great significance. Each triangle within the pyramid holds a particular signature energy. The number four is very important and sacred within the union of the divine feminine and masculine. It holds not only the polarity of the divine masculine and divine feminine, but it also holds the dark feminine and the dark masculine. Forming a complete unification of all polarities.

The purpose of a union is to de-polarize the human nature, bringing our most powerful energies- which are our sexual energies, into a complete sacred union.

Therefore, the initiates in the Temple must go through the initiation process which involves embracing and uniting their light as well as their shadow. Unify their own divinity and Shadow. This is where true healing happens. Where one evolves beyond the lower chakras. Where are all the parts of one's being are merging to form a whole soul.

This unification surpasses old traumas and soul fragmentation that has been caused to a person because of traumas or belief systems that have destroyed one's connection to the divine

THE NUMBER 13

If you add the two numbers that build this one, (3 and 1) you get the number 4. It is a very feminine number. Just like the feminine energy, it has been demonized in our culture, as a wicked number that brings ill luck or darkness.

Number 1, which is a masculine number, stands before the number 3, which is a feminine number. Creating beautiful partnership energy- together form the number 4- the number that represents the divine mother herself.

Work with this number in solitary work, awakening your magical powers and intuition, as well as uniting your own inner feminine and masculine. This number can help you call upon a more aligned lover as well and protect you from people that are not suitable for your path. When you date someone new and considering whether they are the right match, use the power of this number. I will not tell you how. Use your intuition and imagination. Trust yourself.

THE NUMBER 6

The number 6 is a very earthly number. Represents pure balance. A wonderful number to invoke a romantic relationship. Especially relationships that are designed to bring balance and create a higher vibration on the planet.

Doubling the number 3 will bring us number 6- which is expanded, doubled the power of the number 3- and the manifestation of the number 3 in the Physical Realm. So, you can understand how powerful this number is, especially when you write it down 3 times- 666.

The number 6 on its own is already doubling the power of the number 3- and if we write it down 3 times- it is endlessly emanating powers in the physical world. You can use this number to manifest into physicality everything that you want. Makes sense now why it has been used by dark sorcerers, while at the same time the same sorcerers have demonized it and made you think it is evil. No symbol is evil, how humans use it- is. Unfortunately, the dark lords of this planet have been using this number in very malefic ways. Just like many of the sacred symbols and numbers. But do not fear this number. USE IT. Use it correctly. With pure intention.

Please make sure you are using this sequence of numbers with a very pure heart and intentions. You can add this number to your sigil, enhancing its powers.

THE NUMBER 9

This is the number that triples the power of the number 3. This is the number of spiritual awakening and serving the world, humanity, the Mother. A very simple and pure yet extremely powerful number to use when seeking your purpose and desiring to connect with your unique gifts to share with the world. This is the number to use when you are completely ready to become the divine being that you are. It will give you lasting success, eternal connection to the divine, and to your own soul.

This number is patient, it wishes to connect you with the god/goddess within yourself.

This number does not judge, but it is the number that brings judgment to your life so far. It is connected to your karma. It is not a 'punisher' but wishes to bring you into harmony with your own being. Therefore, using this number might feel sometimes like you are being 'judged or punished' - but it merely tries to align you with who you truly are and connect you with your inner wisdom and integrity. So, make sure that you are ready for what this number will create in your life when you use its powers. Make sure you are walking your path with whole integrity in ALL that you do in your everyday life. Make sure you are aligned with your soul and feeling your connection and therefore, effect, on all life. ALL LIFE. This number will bring judgment. As both gifts and karma. It will help you end things you no longer need and enter a new realm of existence. If you honor its power.

THE NUMBER 11

Since the number 1 is a very divine masculine number, the number 11 is the number that brings higher power, alignment with your true self, focus on your mission or purpose, it connects you with higher frequency from a place of commitment to your soul. It can help you with a complete transformation of your eternal power. Whether you are a man or woman, this number connects your purpose with your alignment and commitment of a more masculine force. This number is very focused. Determined. Aligned. It will bring you a clear vision connection to your higher self. If you see this number, it may also be your time to connect with your divine masculine power when it comes to your spiritual commitment to your purpose on your purpose in life. Take physical, intentional actions that are aligned with your soul, spirit, and heart. Actions that are aligned with your words and who you wish to be.

THE NUMBER 22

This number is not used in the temple so much. Even though it adds up to be number 4. The number of the mother herself.

It is mostly used by, shall we say, beginner initiates, who wish to unite their own polarity within them. It is a 'simple' number. Very kind in its energy. It helps those who are just beginning on their path of awakening in a gentler way. If you feel called to this number, use it with joy and allow it to guide you to truth and new knowledge. According to the temple- It is a 'way-shower' to the awakening human.

THE NUMBER 33

Now that you already know that the dark lords have been using the most powerful symbols for malefic ways, you can already guess that this number holds a very special power because it is used very often in your world by dark sorcerers.

This number is used in High Priestess Magic rituals in the temple. Mostly in the lower pyramid- the underground pyramid. It is an extremely feminine number. One that holds the true knowledge, power, and wisdom of the temple itself.

This number has been hijacked by the dark lords for too long.

It is time that we take back the power of this number into our own hands.

It is time to return to the temple and take back the hold of sacred symbols and numbers and use them in a way to transform this reality. It is time to set free the consciousness of mankind. To breakthrough from this prison of the mind.

Therefore, the sisters of the Temple have given permission to all initiates - beginners and advanced to use the number 33 in all their sexual union rituals.

We ask you to place this number on your altar. Draw a circle around it for protection as well as a triangle to give it clear focus. The number is to be drawn with your least used hand- the feminine hand. The circle must be drawn with your masculine hand-the hand you use most. The job of the masculine is to protect. Make sure you draw the circle with love in your heart. No fear. No doubt. Simply love and connection with joy to the temple and your own power.

There is another way to draw this number. And this is the infinity symbol.

When you turn one of the 3's to another Direction, and you have both 3's face each other- you get the infinity symbol- also the number 8. You can draw them both on your altar.

You can also draw the number 8 and have a number three in each of the circles it creates. like this:

THE NUMBER 8

This is the number of eternity. Infinite movement and flow. Great for the divine, sacred, pure sexual union. Used more by twin souls or soul mates to purify their sexual flow, as learned in level 1. Use the image of this number and symbol as you practice your sexual flow breathing exercises.

As mentioned before, when we write the number 3 twice, facing the other- we get the number 8. This represents to our subconscious mind the two, whole, balanced beings, united within their own light and shadow. Feminine and masculine- as they come together, facing one another in sacred union.

THE NUMBER 44

This is of course the sacred number of the mother. Uniting with itself. Partnering with its own Force. Just like the ouroboros who unites with its own body. It is the same type of energy and power that this number holds.

It also adds up to the number 8 of course. This number is less strict with the way to use it. Anytime you use the number for it is a blessing. It is a connection to the mother herself.

Therefore, you may use this number in any way you wish.

I like to use the number tripled- 444.

That, by the way, is why I also charge a specific amount to my programs for example- 1444- it holds the masculine form of commitment from the initiate, followed by a triple force of the Divine mother and blessings of the temple itself. This strengthens commitment between me and my students and blesses our work with the perfect Trinity of the power of the mother. That is why when I work with my initiates in my programs, we are always Guided by the mother herself and the sisters of the Temple, and the transformation of their lives is beyond magical.

PART 4
LOVE OF THE TEMPLE

PURIFICATION & CLEANSING

We have discussed purification and cleansing as preparation for the sexual union in Level 1, but it is important to mention again here as a reminder.

For the people who came for healing or learning in the temple, cleansing and bathing before their rituals were always necessary for the temple. Many men even had to have a long period of initiation before they even met the priestesses, which included a physical as well as symbolic cleansing and daily, deep purification practices.

The human body emits and takes in energy and information non-stop. From air, food, water as well as other people's energy that they emit, their thoughts, and even emotions. Keeping our vessels and energy bodies clean at all times is a basic, important way of life for the one who wishes to be in a strong connection to their higher self and receive pure information- light codes

The priestesses had to keep their bodies pure as well while cultivating divine energy, which is- all the time! The men will not come to have sex with their bodies- but to receive healing and energy from their energy. This kind of work requires one to be at the most pristine state of being always, which keeps the priestess as well as the initiate to be in a constant state of self- awareness, wholesome divinity. In their full potential and power.

The importance of cleansing and purification was seen as a solid foundation in the temple walls, and it was crucial to set up and follow through with effective practice.

We mentioned earlier that the number 33 is used mostly for the initiate men in their time of preparation and cleansing when they are only allowed into the main halls of the temple but not to the deeper chambers.

Use this number in your time of preparation as guided in Level 1 (*Sex Magic Evolution* book), no matter if you are male or female. This number contains all light codes to aid with this journey of self- initiation and reminds you on a subconscious level to take actions and be aware of your regular cleansing on all levels of your being. It will help keep your vessel and energy body pure (as pure as you intent on it being. Remember- you hold all power with your intention and attention).

Keep the main 3 chakras always clear of all blockages. The heart, throat, and sexual centers.

These, when remaining pure and strong, will lead the sexual flow up to the third eye in the best way and help your awakening process.

Consuming only light foods is vital for your purification (and beyond). Light foods are mostly raw (uncooked) fruits, vegetables, nuts seeds, and herbs. But you can enjoy cooked foods as long as it is plant based. All that grows and is given freely from the earth.

Eating animals and animal by-products (which is a form of the darkest baneful magic of blood sacrifice) will keep your physical body, energy body & emotional body not only in a low vibration place because of the actual flesh and blood of the animal that is toxic for all our body systems functions, but it will keep you in a state of perpetual trauma & fear which in turn, make you easily controlled and keep you aligned with low-frequency energies. These energies can manifest in a form of a demon, disease, illness (of body or mind), and being in fear, lack, pain in many ways. Most of all, this blocks you from your authentic spirit, highest soul, open clear heart, and it absolutely blocks your divine sexual flow and life force.

Make sure you are free of alcohol, which opens an immediate doorway to lower dimensions and demonic entities. Make sure you are surrounded by people who mirror the vibration of the human YOU wish to become. Make sure you make every daily decision from a place of heart alignment and integrity- this keeps the 'purity' of your mind and self.

And most of all- men- follow your heart, and women- follow your womb.
Connect once more to the wisdom, power, and love you hold within the cells of your light vessel.

TWIN FLAMES

THE HARSH TRUTH ABOUT TWIN FLAME

The concept of twin flames has been overly misused in our new age community.

It became a symbol on its own. A symbol of pure love, powerful eternal love which most humans dream of having. But this symbol of the twin flame has, like many of the sacred symbols, been demolished as well.

Very few understand and know what a twin flame is. The sisters would like me to mention this now because it is important that humans know this and begin using the power of the twin flame as it should be used. And stop using it when they don't need to.

The reason that the idea that was formed in our world about twin flames holds so much power within our psyche is that it does hold some truth to it. Hollywood, as well as the new age world, have pictured an image to us that actually holds the true meaning of a twin flame. Therefore, it speaks to our soul so much and we all crave this kind of connection.

We all have many soulmates during our lives. Almost everyone we meet in our life is our soul mate. Whether we encounter them for 5 minutes, five years, or for the length of our entire lifetime. They are here to awaken the part of our soul, push certain buttons if you will, and activate a specific frequency within us.

A twin flame connection is a unique connection. Not everyone is a twin flame. Many people want to be twin flames, but they are not twin flames and they do not have twin flames. Not in a sense that we have believed to be at least.

Every human is in fact a twin flame for themselves. Meaning that the true union of every human individual must happen first within themselves and only in themselves. The divine feminine and divine masculine within each one of us must be united in order to activate the light codes of the power of the individual human being. This is the true energetic work of the Temple.

A few individuals on our planet, are in fact twin flames in the way that society believes this term to mean. Meaning they have another counterpart outside themselves, another soul if you will- that they are deeply connected to in a way that is far beyond the way and the power of an actual human being.

Most twin flames are not originated on earth. Many of them are volunteers on this planet. They came from other dimensions and planets to help humankind in the Awakening process, and therefore they needed a counterpart to help them in this very heavy, difficult mission.

THE STORY OF THE TWINS

Two bodies. Two polarities. Positive and negative. Come together, aligned for the sake of a mutual purpose. One soul, split into two parts- in spirit and body – male and female.

Twin flames, as opposed to what many believe today are very rare. It is a sacred and powerful bond which most humans today cannot hold. Many want to believe they are twins and confuse the term with soul mate and ideas of romance, but twin flames come from a specific dimension and hold light codes of the blue-violet flame. Their cells are connected to a piece of specific coded information brought here through the cells of their DNA for the purpose of aiding human ascension.

Twins have the ability to see through the false light and dark sorcerers' agenda. That is why they are psychically targeted from the moment they are born.

They have the natural ability to live in a few dimensions at the same time, mostly because they are NOT together in the body at the same time. They work many times throughout different dimensions. Only about half of twin flames actually meet in this lifetime in the physical body. They do only if they are fully prepared for each other or if their mission calls for it. If they are not, they will continue to do their work together through other energetic means. They can have a full relationship through dreamtime or energetically feel and communicate with each other. Though this is hard for them, they know that this is the best way for them to do their work on this plane.

In their proper state, they are connected to the mother/ creator source and embody true care for this world, love, and compassion to all beings. This doesn't mean they are perfect, they still live as humans, but they live knowing their connection to all life and if their actions are not aligned with their soul, they feel an immediate shift in their energy and can even get sick. Twin flames will live as what we call- 'vegans' because they feel and know their connection to all life. If they are not awakened or connected to their divine alchemy, they may eat animals and that will keep them even farther from their true power and of their flame connection.

The dark has been destroying and attacking our DNA on many levels because this destroys our true power and ability to receive light codes (information). The twin's work is to guide humanity into seeing that the ascension must happen within. The codes they hold 'push' humans around them to go within and find their own inner flame. The blue-violet flame that will remind them of their inner journey that must be taken to reach ascension.

The dark wants to keep this earth on a low frequency and the twins are here to help awaken the flame of energy in humans. Unlike different volunteer souls that are here for different reasons, mainly to elevate the frequency on the planet.
There are much fewer twin souls then there are volunteer souls/star-seeds, though all twins in a way, ARE star-seeds/ volunteers.

THE LAW OF GENDER

Twin flames that are incarnated together in the body are ALWAYS- male and female. There are no twin flames that are the same sex. This may be hard for some to hear, but the twin flame soul must come together in the physical realm in pure perfect physical alchemy (semen and egg). They align with the natural laws of this universe, including the law of gender.

They both must hold the perfect divine masculine and feminine in every way. This is going to be hard to accept for some people who believe in the false concept of gender fluidity that the new age movement has been marketing as truth. When it comes to a sacred sexual flow and alchemy, A divine masculine in its pure form cannot be contained within a female's body. And the divine feminine in her pure form cannot be contained in the body of a male. This is a lie and manipulation of the dark agenda that has heavily influenced the new age community with the aim to destroy our sacred sexual power and connection. And we must stop and understand that the embodiment of our divine polarity in our gender is a gift that we must use to create a sacred sexual union.

Therefore, the dark agenda has been also targeting human relationships and destroying the sacredness of coming together and the idea of the sacred marriage. The sacred marriage, (which we discuss in level 1), is not about any religious ceremony, but about a divine soul union that births light into the world. A divine couple can naturally and easily bring light codes into this realm. This is why the law of gender is so important here on this realm.

Same-sex partners can absolutely have an amazing soul connection and bring the purest love energy to their environment-magic I have witnessed various times, but I am sorry to say that true alchemy will not occur, for pure sexual alchemy requires the sexual fluids of both male and female body. And that is why twin flames will always incarnate as both male and female because they must create this alchemy.

Each partner must be ready. Must have gone through the preparation in the form of shadow work, body cleansing, and aligned with their own (light-shadow) polarity and gender and any other universal law that exists. Only then they can come together and hold the codes they were meant to bring.

This is one of the reasons that so few twin flames are actually together in the body – because they are not ready. They have been programmed and confused by the many false ideas of this world that have manipulated our natural powers. Most twin flames don't know they are twin flames. And please don't believe the romantic idea about them. it is all soul-consuming to be a twin flame, and what is better is to be a whole, awakened, conscious human ready to create a sacred union and enjoy it! this human life is a unique gift not many in the cosmos get to experience. Do the work to be the perfect vessel for it and create a sacred union in your life. you can even bring more light into this world than any twin flame who is not ready to do so. We need you now!

THE GIFTS AND RESPONSIBILITY OF THE TWINS

Twins can see and connect to the many levels of reality unless their bodies are very acidic from animal products, alcohol, drugs, trauma, etc..

They are connected to all their own selves in other levels of reality in which they exist simultaneously for the sole reason of helping this physical reality.

they must use their gifts but their work on this planet is harder than other humans. Most humans cannot handle this energy the twins hold. This is not something you want to be. Respect the work of the twins and stop labeling every boyfriend/ girlfriend/ partner as your twin. They are probably not. Focus instead on your inner path, align with your soul, and find YOUR signature here. YOUR path. And this will empower you.

Twin flames shift and change constantly. They always evolve, try new things, aim to learn who they are in the moment, and become their better version. It is almost like they are in a constant state of shadow work and self-observation and awareness since they always can be both in the shadow and light simultaneously. They know they must be always aligned because they naturally need to bring this alignment into the flame they carry together. The idea of romantic love is needed, for it attracts them to each other, but it is the deep soul connection and purpose that keeps them together. Truth is the glue they are bound with, not illusion.

Like many volunteer souls on the planet, twin flames know from childhood that this is 'not their home'. They as well feel like they are here for a while, for a reason, and are not a part of the human karmic cycle. That is why it is hard for them to be around many humans and why they do not wish to create any unnecessary karma- like volunteer souls- which they feel will keep them in this dimension. So, they are grounded within the human experience but usually do not want to have children for example (which causes tremendous karma) or get too involved in their human society. They are a part of it, but not of it. this is ironic because this sense deep sense of detaching from the karmic human experience is usually what is stopping them from being in relationships in the first place.

They feel wonderful romantic love if they are together in the body, but they do not place much significance on it for they know their bond must stay pure for the light it holds.

Twin flames will not even want to use the term twin flames. They know this term is even too small to encompass who they are. It is like the modern-day shamans who call themselves shamans. Real shamans don't even call themselves shamans. Do you see my point?

We must grow up. Truly take responsibility for who we are and not use labels or a nice wrapping to escape who we truly are. We must connect with our soul so much that we need no label, and we just walk our soul path naturally.

Using this term with no respect for its meaning also puts you in danger of clinging and holding on to unhealthy relationships just because you really want to believe that they are your twin flame.

I see this all the time! in fact, I've been there myself.

Being a twin is not a walk in the park and you may hold different, unique, important light codes and are here on your own mission but you are not aligned with it because you are caught up with labeling yourself as a label such as -'twin flame.'

All that is important to remember is not to label yourself as a twin, whether you are one or not. That takes your focus from who you really are. Forget the label of twin flame unless you know with every part of your being, after reading this part, that you are in fact a twin. If you are one of those who have held on to the story you are a twin, take the time for self-initiation and fully go within to get to know who YOU truly are and not the 'self' that you thought you were. Empty yourself at this moment in time and re-learn yourself. Ask yourself: "why do I think I am a twin? What did that story give me or how did it serve me so far?" "Who would I be without this story?"

Be brutally honest with yourself. The truth will set you free.

I know that for some of you this sounds too harsh, but I am here to give you the truth and set you free. That is my soul's path, and I will walk it no matter what. I am not here to be loved. I am already love.

I am here to awaken. And this for me- is how I truly can love you and show my love for you. You deserve absolute freedom, with all it entails and you deserve pure joy in life, in love, in sex…

The full self-initiation with all the guidelines in level 1 (*Sex Magic Evolution* book) will give you a clear knowing whether you are or are not a twin flame.

You must purify and cleanse your entire being first and go through the period of shadow work, inner alchemy, and full awakening in the 3rd, 4th, and 5th dimensions to KNOW this for sure. Otherwise, you will be fooling yourself with the fantastic ideas of twin flames as they are presented by the new age movement or Hollywood movies and you will be robbing yourself pure joy. The job of the twin is HARD. It is not something one wants to take on so easily. It is, for most twins, a lifetime of loneliness because the other twin is in another realm, or it will take them long to be ready for each other. It is a life of commitment to a higher purpose and almost a constant state of sacrificing one's pleasures for the sake of the path and the mission.

THE TWIN SOUL AGREEMENT

Many people today hold the extremely misguided idea that twin flames must experience pain, hurt, separation before they Unite. They also believe that all twin flames are going to be united in the physical body and experience the sort of magical romantic love you see in the Hollywood movies.

Those people are going to find the truth very difficult to believe and will even resist it very strongly. I know I resisted myself as well, and the truth, the way I received it from The Sisters of the Temple, which hold the knowledge of the true twin flame connection- is this:

Twin flames do not have to encounter each other in a physical body. They, in fact, most choose not to Incarnate together in a physical body in the third dimension. This is true more and more as time on our planet goes by and the energies here are not only too destructive for the twins but in fact, if twins work in both dimensions at the same time- meaning- one twin in the physical earth and one on another realm, they can, sometimes- do their work and assist this planet even better.

Again, this is true only for some and it is truer for this generation of twins than the one before.

Twin flames are two souls or one Soul who have a mission together, who hold a third energy together- like the symbol of the triangle in the sex magic temple.

They hold specific energy TOGETHER and that energy is more than them combined. More than just the sum of who they are and their self-desires from each other and from their relationship.

They are living for a mission and a reason and a purpose that is greater than them. In a way, they may sacrifice their own physical, sexual, and romantic needs for a higher purpose and for their work together in this realm and other realms.

Therefore, they do not have to incarnate in a physical body together. In fact, it is better, for some, as I mentioned before- that they don't.

When one twin chooses to remain in another dimension, they in fact are helping the twin who chose to come into incarnation into a physical body. The work of a twin is extremely difficult. Especially for those who chose to volunteer on this planet at this moment. Therefore, they will do their job better if one is assisting from another dimension, helping the physical twin in raising their vibration, protecting them energetically and physically, and guiding them in their path.

The Romantic ideal of love and romantic connection which we see in films and fairy tales is absolutely a part of a twin flame connection, but it is not all of it. Far from it. It is merely a small part of their connection and Union.

The love connection and the sexual experience that they can experience can shatter the world completely. This is another reason why twin flames choose not to come together in a physical body because their energy could in fact be too much if they do not know how to use it wisely. Many human beings today believe they are living with their 'twin flame' but in fact, they are in a complete soulmate relationship. A very beautiful, powerful, love relationship, but not a twin flame one.

The romantic love story is one we all subconsciously seek and desire, but this romantic love story is just a little piece of the Twin Flame relationship. It is the icing on the cake if you will. But it is not what gives the nourishment and power to this dimension. It is not what they truly seek from their bond.

What real twin flames seek from their Union is pure power. Power is not bad. Power is power. It all depends on how you use it. Twins seek power in order to help. Power in order to elevate and expand consciousness. Power in order to unite human beings with their own soul. Power to set free the mind of humans at this point. They seek to raise vibrations, to share knowledge. To bring light. Each set of twins do this in their own unique signature way, but the feeling and commitment to the path are the same.

A huge piece of it is our individual work and shadow work and spiritual work that we do by ourselves before we come together and uniting with our twin flame and that is almost half of the work already. So, the person that is not doing any work on himself, REAL and I mean- REAL WORK- on themselves- are not a twin flame. They want to be one, but they are not, and they do not hold or live the energy of a twin flame.

LET GO OF THE STORY

I invite you to do something, whether you are or are not a twin flame. Get the story out of your mind- the story about twin flames- because it is hindering you in your expansion and in your work here on Earth. And if you ARE a twin, it is in fact, hindering you from connecting with your true twin.

I know this because I have been there, so I want to shake you off of it because I want you to begin to really focus on your own soul expansion and your own mission here on Earth. I want you to first unite the divine feminine and masculine within yourself. That is the true awakening of a twin flame energy anyway. And even if you are not a twin flame of another soul, you can still do a twin flame work within yourself right now. You can awaken light codes that are dormant within you. You can bring more light into this realm right now.

If you are a twin, your twin will find you or you will find them. And again, this union does not have to happen in a physical body. Because the union that you both share is an inter-dimensional Union. It is beyond space and time. Even your sexual union will be the best sex you will ever have. Because it surpasses the limitations of the physical body. It is a connection of soul-body- mind-heart as one.

Let go of the idea or the stories you may have on twin flames. Focus on your mission right now on earth. Focus on who you are and who you want to become. Focus on uniting both polarities within yourself in their divine essence. Masculine and feminine as well as your light and shadow (as you are guided in Level 1). Focus on your own soul expansion.

If you are twin - call upon your twin. Speak to them. Your twin may need help somewhere. Or you may need the help of your twin. Form a connection, no matter where you are right now in the ether. No matter if you are together in the body or not. But do not let it stop you and do not let it take your focus from where you are right now. If you are a twin, know your twin wishes you to focus on your mission and expanding your consciousness. That is, in fact, the best way to connect with your twin.
Because the union that happens within yourself- the union of your own divine masculine and feminine- is the only union that actually matters. Twin Flame or not. First, you are your own twin flame. First, you must create the contact in the union within yourself.
If you are a twin, you are meant to unite with your twin whether on this dimension or another. Trust the union and let it go for now. Unite both polarities within yourself and focus on your own expansion.

Twins hold and work with the Violet/blue Flame. The flame of the Soul, the flame of the soul body. Twin flames work together more in the etheric realm. They have their individual work on this planet in a physical body, yet they unite and do their energetic work together as a team in the etheric realms.

If you do not have the ability to work in a few dimensions at the same time. If you cannot jump through timelines naturally and do spiritual work in the etheric realm, I am sorry to say, you are not a twin flame. It is not good or bad it just means you have a different mission here on Earth. Maybe even a bigger one.

It means you have a mission to do by yourself which contains more of your physical body and your physical actions as well as your emotions which hold a tremendous amount of power as a human being. You are here to ground new energy. This is in fact good news, because you may enjoy the wonderful romantic love actually more than twin flames can in most cases. You have more of the freedom in the physical realm when it comes to romantic love and the space to enjoy it in all its shapes and forms. In a way, you can have more 'fun' than twins can... all depends of course on your soul's divine path, which you will find and know when you truly- KNOW THYSELF.

When twin flames finish their work together in this physical realm, they usually remain for a while in the etheric realm together. In a way to finish up the details of their work together on Earth, to solidify their work before they move on to other dimensions and release themselves from the karma of the planet if they wish to do so, or they may wish to come back to another incarnation and continue their work in the physical body in a different way. Even go to other planes of existence to do other work together. They are completely free and sovereign from the cycle of karma of this planet. And that is another reason why one twin chooses to not be in a physical body- because this helps them to remain above and outside the cycle of karma that is imprisoning so many of human beings.

The physical plane is very difficult for twin flames and volunteers in general, therefore, many twin flames feel the physical aching of not being with their twin flame in a physical body, but as soon as they form a true connection to their twin flame, spiritually and energetically, they feel tremendous relief and freedom and they begin to do their work more powerfully and with more focus.

I speak from experience, and I hope this gives you hope and inspiration.

This is a real issue for twin flames, and it is a great challenge, but we must remember we chose to come here in this way for a specific reason. Once we connect to our true soul's mission there is a huge shift and this aching yearning takes a different shape in our experience. It becomes the fuel that drives us, the light of inspiration that guides us. the wind beneath our wings.

We must delete the program of this world and the ideas of romantic love the way it is portrayed to us in this society and see beyond the illusion.

Trust me, I know that this is a very difficult reality to accept for many. That some twins will always be separated in the body while in this world. For it took me many years to accept it myself, but the mission and raising the frequency on planet earth is what matters most and really this life is fleeting. We will unite with our twin and enjoy a tremendous amount of love with them at some point in our existence. Whether it be in this dimension or another.

This truth could be liberating and empowering for those who are twins. Especially for those who are volunteers from other planes of existence.

And this doesn't mean you cannot enjoy a beautiful, supportive, passionate love relationship with a physical partner. You absolutely should if the right one comes along. In fact, your twin may help you in finding a physical partner who will be the best team-mate for this ride. They may bring them to you and you can feel your twin's love through them.

WALK-IN TWIN-FLAME SOULS

Twin flames may choose to join their partner in a physical body. What we may know as a walk-in. That is very rare to happen, for it requires a tremendous amount of shifts in the energy of the body itself and the reality around the physical body of the person. Not many can handle that shift while still in physical form. But it does happen.

A walk-in is a soul that walks in -literally - into a physical body of another human being within the time frame of their physical life. Meaning, the energy of a soul can walk in and incarnate into another physical body, not in the time of the birth of the body, but at some time during the lifetime itself.

If this occurs and the twins choose to unite in a physical body during this lifetime, it most likely will happen in the later time in a human's life, where the mission and their work together has been almost completed. This will only happen in a time in their lives where they are grounded within themselves enough, where they are focused on their mission enough to not let the physical romantic union distract them from what really matters.

This means, that they are going to unite when they are older in age, more mature, and have accomplished much of their mission together already.

THE NUMBER OF TWIN FLAMES ON EARTH

The number of twin flames on planet Earth at any given time is dependent on the amount of darkness currently happening on the planet. At this moment for example (the year 2020) the number of twin flames is closer to 3 million, for the darkness, it is rising more and more.

According to the information I have received from the sisters of the temple, Approximately A thousand years ago for example the number of twins was about 100,000.

When the earth needs more light and elevated energy, more volunteers will be called, and more twin flames will be created and formed.

A twin flame is in fact a structure of divine feminine and masculine, working perfectly together within the vibrations of this dimension. For they know that this dimension is one of polarity, and before they come here, they know that they must work in perfect unison of their divine feminine and masculine in order to do their work in the best way possible and to raise the frequency on planet Earth.

CREATE YOUR OWN SYMBOL HERE:

create your own sigil that holds your divine spirit essence, inner wisdom, and soul purpose.

Write down your statement of all these things and use the method of creating a sigil from Level 1 (Sex Magic Evolution)

TO THE TRUE LOVE-MAKERS

Find your gift. Do it your way.
With your emotions, divine pure sexual force, and truth.
Spoken and formed into matter, guided by your spirit, your heart, and womb.
The truth that is birthed by your connection to ALL life.
Integrate your light and shadow, all fragmented parts of who you are and always have been, and from that whole place- CHOOSE who you want to be. Which character you are now in this story we are all co-creating together.

DEAR SOUL FAMILY

If you enjoyed this book & were inspired by these words, please write a review on Amazon, and let me know your thoughts. This supports my work.

Thank you for connecting, with me, and the temple.

Love, *Luna Ora*

THE SEX MAGIC SCHOOL OF ISIS AND LILITH

BOOKS

Sex Magic Evolution

Symbols of Sex Magic

The Sex Priestess Manual

Promised In Fire- (Fiction)

PROGRAMS

The Goddess Return

The God-Man

The Sex Priestess Initiation Path

CLASSES

Candle Sex Magic

Creating Magical Children

Potion Making

WWW.MOTHERISRISING.COM

ABOUT THE AUTHOR

Luna Ora was born and raised in Israel.
a servant of the mother & a soul explorer, she found her path to the temple and is now a spiritual teacher and the founder of the sex magic school of ISIS and LILITH, where she awakens humans with occult wisdom and creating real love makers on earth.

Luna Ora
A servant of the mother

Made in the USA
Las Vegas, NV
13 September 2024

95221623R00095